What would Keynes do?

Tejvan Pettinger

What would Keynes do?

How the greatest **economists** would solve your everyday problems

Tejvan Pettinger

An Hachette UK Company
www.hachette.co.uk

First published in Great Britain in 2018 by Cassell,
a division of Octopus Publishing Group Ltd
Carmelite House
50 Victoria Embankment
London EC4Y 0DZ
www.octopusbooks.co.uk

ISBN 978 1 84403 980 7

A CIP catalogue record for this book is available from the British Library.

Printed and bound in China

10 9 8 7 6 5 4 3 2 1

Editorial Director: Trevor Davies
Senior Editor: Pollyanna Poulter
Copy Editor: Alison Wormleighton
Art Director: Yasia Williams
Designer: Ella McLean
Production Controller: Sarah Kulasek-Boyd

Contents

Introduction   **6**

Chapter 1: Life choices   8

Is it OK to be selfish? • Should I park in an illegal parking space and risk a fine? • What is the secret of happiness? • How can I resolve disputes with neighbours? • Is it better to gamble on the lottery or gamble by having no insurance? • Should I make an effort to turn off all the electric lights? • Should I bother to recycle? • How can I lose weight (through economics)? What is the optimal number of children to have?

Chapter 2: The consumer   48

If I enjoy drinking beer, how much should I drink? • Can I trust a second-hand car salesman? How do we best manage common resources? • Should I pay to go to the front of the line? How much should we give to charity? • Should I give a gift or money for a Christmas present? Should I favour buying local goods? • How can I get a good deal when shopping?

Chapter 3: Work   84

Should I go to college/university? • Is it worth taking a promotion if it involves working long hours? • How do I motivate my fellow workers? • Do I benefit or suffer from immigration? Should I give up my secure job and work for myself? • How can I get a pay rise? • How can I be a good manager of people? • Should I run my business just for profit?

Chapter 4: Finance   120

How do I beat the market? • How do I survive inflation? • How can I make my small business more profitable? • How much should I put into retirement savings? • How do I avoid getting caught by financial bubbles? • How much personal debt should I take on?

Chapter 5: Politics   148

Should I vote for a political party that promises to cut my income taxes? • Should I boycott goods made in sweatshop factories? • Should I support government subsidies for a local firm facing bankruptcy? • Will I be better off with tariffs on imports? • Should I welcome parking charges in my street and city? • Should I support the legalization of drugs? • Should I worry about my government getting into debt? • Should we worry about rising inequality? • Should health care be private or public?

Bibliography   **184**
Index   **188**
Acknowledgments   **192**

Introduction

Although economic issues have been around since the dawn of time, economics as a distinct and influential subject only really emerged in the late 18th century as society moved from an agrarian economy to the brave new world of industrial capitalism. Pioneers such as Adam Smith and David Ricardo reflected on this period of rapid change and examined fundamental aspects of the economy, such as free markets and international trade. This led to a basic economic framework, known as classical economics.

However, though economists may agree on some fundamentals, the subject attracts a huge diversity of opinion on how we should harness the power of economic forces. Indeed, any particular economic problem can be seen from very different perspectives – if there is one thing that unites economists, it is the awareness that there is always another point of view.

One of the most influential economists of the 20th century was John Maynard Keynes. An original thinker, brilliant intellect and man of supreme self-confidence, he came into his own during the crisis of the 1930s Great Depression. While many floundered and wondered why economic theories were not working like they were supposed to, Keynes threw out the textbooks and came up with his own. His *General Theory of Employment, Interest and Money* was dense, hard to read and not without inherent contradictions, but his vision enabled him to view economics from a fresh perspective, seeing how governments could play a role in stabilizing the temperamental forces of capitalism. Keynes was one of the most brilliant economists of the century, though not without his ardent critics.

More than money

As a general rule, economics is concerned with such matters as economic growth, industrial efficiency and inflation – the kind of issues that can seem peripheral to our daily lives. Yet in recent decades, some economists have broadened the scope of the subject and tried to apply its ideas to aspects of everyday life, from crime and punishment to family life and the ethics of queue-jumping. The Nobel Laureate Gary Becker was particularly influential in pushing the boundaries and showing how economics could potentially illuminate seemingly mundane life choices.

This new strand of applied economics has been complemented by the rise of behavioural economics, a field that has blurred the boundaries with other social sciences. By examining how psychological and social influences impact our economic decisions, it has created a new framework for examining the perennial questions of economics. Pioneers in this field such as Daniel Kahneman and Richard Thaler suggest that humans are much more unpredictable and irrational than the abstract models of economics textbooks might suggest (something that non-economists may have known all along).

Something of a revolution

In expanding the subject in recent decades, both Gary Becker and the behavioural economists certainly made it easier to write this particular book, which involves examining how different economists might approach everyday questions. If *What Would Keynes Do?* had been written in the 1960s, it would have been a lot shorter, as many of the ideas and theories it covers are relatively recent. This is one of the interesting things about studying economics – it is so fast-changing. Yet the legendary figures like Adam Smith, Alfred Marshall, John Maynard Keynes and Milton Friedman still make regular appearances. New economic theories can challenge long-held orthodoxy, but do not entirely overthrow its insights.

A fresh approach to the world around you

In considering a range of practical questions about life, this book looks at the theories and philosophies

of a broad spectrum of economic thinkers – from free-market ideologues to Marxists to the new generation of economists outside the mainstream. Whether you agree or disagree with their seemingly disparate ideas, hopefully it will make you aware of some of the many different ways we can approach the same economic problems and perhaps see ordinary issues in a new light.

Life choices

Page 10: Is it OK to be selfish?

Page 14: Should I park in an illegal parking space and risk a fine?

Page 19: What is the secret of happiness?

Page 23: How can I resolve disputes with neighbours?

B3CK3R

Page 28: Is it better to gamble on the lottery or gamble by having no insurance?

Page 32: Should I make an effort to turn off all the electric lights?

Page 36: Should I bother to recycle?

Page 40: How can I lose weight (through economics)?

Page 44: What is the optimal number of children to have?

Chapter 1

Is it OK to be selfish?

Adam Smith • David Ricardo • William Stanley Jevons • Karl Marx
Frank Knight • John Kenneth Galbraith • Robert H Frank
Friedrich Hayek • Ludwig von Mises • Milton Friedman • Arthur Pigou

We are brought up to feel that being selfish is morally dubious. Yet mainstream economic theory holds out the proposition that pursuing one's own self-interest can benefit the whole society. Is it really the case that a self-interested approach magically increases net social welfare or should we be suspicious of a subject like economics that seems to preach self-interest and profit maximization?

The question gets to the heart of many debates within economics, so it is appropriate to start with the father of economics, **Adam Smith** (1723–90). In his seminal work, *The Wealth of Nations* (1776), Smith laid the framework for *classical economics* which suggested that if individuals pursue their own selfish interests it can maximize the welfare of society. If we buy the cheapest goods, we reward the most efficient firms. In the pursuit of profit, an entrepreneur provides both employment and the goods consumers need.

This is the magic of the free market and the invisible hand that transforms our self-interest into mutually beneficial transactions. Economic pioneers such as the British economists **David Ricardo** (1772–1823) and **William Stanley Jevons** (1835–82) introduced into their economic theories the concept of a rational man seeking to maximize his own utility – i.e., get maximum value for minimum expenditure. In their world of theoretical economics, this approach of *utility maximization* fortuitously led to an optimal allocation of resources. This created a powerful tradition in economics which assumed that pursuit of self-interest led to an efficient allocation of resources and increase in economic welfare.

However, this myopic view of a free market utopia has definitely not been shared by all economists. Critics of capitalism have suggested that following self-interest could be unfair to poorer members of society, who have less power and privilege. **Karl Marx** (1818–83) denounced the self-interest of capitalists, arguing that it led to exploitation of the weakest in society. *Free market economics* assumes that different agents have equal bargaining power and that in competitive markets the pursuit of self-interest leads to a "fair" equilibrium, but for Karl Marx this

"the most violent, mean and malignant passions of the human breast, the Furies of private interest"
Karl Marx

assumption was invalid. He argued that power and influence enabled the capitalist to selfishly squeeze out toil from workers, who had little choice in the matter. To Marx, selfishness was one of the worst aspects of capitalism.

Indirect benefits – for some

Nevertheless, classical economists have felt that in general a free market and the premise of supporting rational self-interest were preferable to other systems for the distribution of resources. For example, the American economist **Frank Knight** (1885–1972) argued that private enterprise, in which people seek their own self-interest, can solve most problems more efficiently than the government. Knight noted how entrepreneurs take risks so they can gain profit but in the process create jobs and wealth for others in society. In other words, pursuit of self-interest can be an effective means of wealth creation that benefits others in society.

However, this view of free markets and self-interest benefiting all in society is criticized by those who argue that the supposed *trickle-down effect* in reality seldom trickles down to the poorest. The Canadian-born economist **John Kenneth Galbraith** (1908–2006) argued that trickle-down economics was tried in the Gilded Age (at the beginning of the 20th century). He said that at the time it had been aptly described as "horse and sparrow theory" because, he explained, "If you feed the horse enough oats, some will pass through to the road for the sparrows". In other words, maximizing wealth, especially in the presence of

monopoly power, doesn't help everyone in society and is likely to increase inequality and a sense of unfairness.

Side effects of pursuing self-interest

The American economist **Robert H Frank** (b. 1945) has gone farther, arguing that economics encourages people to reject cooperation and generosity and think more from the perspective of self-interest. Frank has also found that studying economics tends to make you more selfish as you become influenced by the dominant

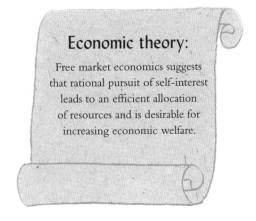

Economic theory:

Free market economics suggests that rational pursuit of self-interest leads to an efficient allocation of resources and is desirable for increasing economic welfare.

Trickle-down economics

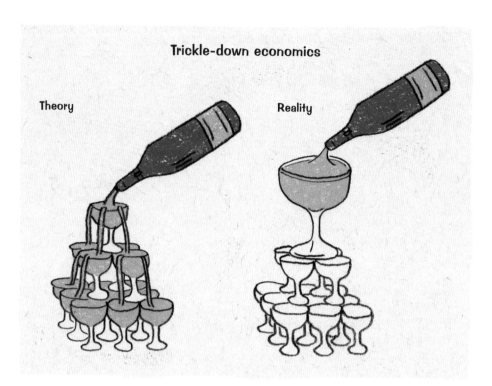

Theory

Reality

self-interest theory. In other words holding up self-interest as an ideal influences our behaviour for the worse.

Defenders of free market economics, such as the Austrian–British economist and winner of a Nobel Memorial Prize **Friedrich Hayek** (1899–1992), claim that it is a false equivalence to argue that the pursuit of self-interest means we approve of selfishness. When men pursue their self-interest, it may involve cultivating their better natures. Adam Smith, while admitting the usefulness of the market mechanism, was also a moral philosopher who hoped man would aspire to more than mere self-interest. Although Smith is viewed as the father of economics, he was aware of the negative aspects of monopoly power and how the pursuit of self-interest could cause social problems and an unfair distribution of resources.

Some *libertarian* economists, such as the Austrian–American **Ludwig von Mises** (1881–1973) and the American **Milton Friedman** (1912–2006), argue for free

"We have always known that heedless self-interest was bad morals; we know now that it is bad economics"
Franklin Delano Roosevelt

> *"There are no irreconcilable conflicts between selfishness and altruism, between economics and ethics, between the concerns of the individual and those of society"*
> Ludwig von Mises

markets precisely because they believe in the absence of government regulation, with the result that people are more likely to cooperate with their neighbours, which promotes social interaction that is mutually beneficial. Libertarians call this *spontaneous order* and point to the numerous organizations that have formed from civil society. In other words, the absence of government intervention encourages people to relate their self-interest to the wider interests of the local community and nation. Von Mises had no doubt that the pursuit of selfish interests could benefit society.

However, if classical economics can make a convincing case for encouraging selfish actions within a competitive free market, there is still the problem of *external costs*, or *externalities* (unintentional consequences of economic activities affecting third parties). The British economist **Arthur Pigou** (1877–1959), in *The Economics of Welfare* (1920), noted how many actions can cause *spillover effects* for other people. For example, the production of electricity by burning fossil fuels causes the external costs, or *negative externalities*, of global warming, acid rain and polluted air. Thus, pursuing our own self-interest can lead to potentially devastating costs to the earth and future generations. This is an idea taken up by environmental economists, who stress that environmental concerns should outweigh our selfish materialistic desires.

Making a decision:

In some areas of commerce and business, free market economists such as Friedman and von Mises are correct that pursuing self-interest can lead to overall benefit for society. However, you may also agree with Pigou and Frank that considering only self-interest is not enough, and that we need to consider our economic impact on other people and the environment; otherwise our selfishness can be damaging to ourselves and society.

13

Should I park in an illegal parking space and risk a fine?

Gary Becker • Jeremy Bentham • Thomas Hobbes • Pierre Bourdieu

We have all been in the situation of arriving late to a meeting and finding our problems compounded by a lacking of parking spaces. We drive furiously around the block looking for somewhere to park but to no avail. To make it worse, there are some nice available spaces – but, just where it would be most convenient, parking is prohibited, by double yellow lines, a spot for disabled drivers only, a threat of wheel clamping or whatever. If we stick to the letter of the law, we may have to drive away and waste more time. By the time we've found a space, parked and run back to the meeting, we're late, sweaty and irritated and, as an external cost, have helped to increase congestion in city centres.

The Nobel Laureate American economist **Gary Becker** (1930–2014) was faced with this dilemma as a young man in the early 1960s, when he was late for an examination of a doctoral student at Columbia University. Using economic analysis, Becker quickly weighed up the pros and cons and decided to park in an illegal space. He calculated that there was a probability of getting a parking fine but that this potential cost was less than the cost of finding a legal but more distant space and arriving even later. He went to the interview, came out afterwards and was relieved to find no parking ticket.

The economics underlying this experience led Becker to investigate the economics behind everyday decisions, particularly with regard to the cost/benefit analysis of criminal action. What is the logic of Becker's decision to park illegally? Suppose there is a $100 fine for illegal parking, but you estimate that the probability of getting

caught is 20%. In this case, the expected cost of parking illegally is $20. If you park illegally every day, that is the average you will end up paying.

However, the important thing is to also put a cost on searching for a correct parking space. If you are meeting a lawyer who is charging you $200 an hour, even a 15-minute delay would cost you $50. In addition, finding a legal space would waste your time and leave you flustered, and there is a degree of uncertainty over how long it would take. The illegal spot removes all that doubt, frustration and time loss, and replaces them with another gamble – whether or not you will get a parking ticket.

The greatest happiness of the greatest number

An economist who takes a rational view would weigh up the cost of parking

illegally against the cost of arriving late. This attitude would have gained the approval of the founder of *utilitarianism*, the English philosopher and economist **Jeremy Bentham** (1748–1832), who argued that we should take decisions on the basis of increasing happiness in society. If we park illegally, we save ourselves time and also make the person waiting for our meeting happy. It is possible we may get a ticket but, overall, the gamble is worth taking. Furthermore, if we do get a ticket, this $100 is not lost to society; it will lead to higher revenues for the local government and, other things being equal, enable lower taxes for everyone else. If we waste time driving around the block looking for legal spaces, we cause external costs to other users by increasing congestion.

Therefore, from a utilitarian perspective, we should ignore the rules and park straightaway to save everyone the hassle. So far, this sounds a very one-sided justification for parking illegally. It seems that everyone wins from the situation. But think again: why are the spaces illegal in the first place? Perhaps the parking space would restrict traffic flow. In this case, parking illegally would cause external costs to other drivers. Perhaps the illegal space is reserved for the disabled. If you take the last disabled spot, it may be good for you but someone who really needs it might come along later and be unable to park. From a utilitarian perspective, that would diminish economic welfare.

What if everyone did it?

Another issue about illegal parking is that there is an element of the problem known as "The Tragedy of the Commons". In 1833 the British economist William Forster Lloyd (1794–1852) noted that a common (land with public rights of use) could easily be overused through overgrazing. This would cause a situation in which individual actions have led to over-exploitation of a natural resource. Does the "Tragedy of the Commons" have any relation to our dilemma concerning parking illegally?

"I calculated the likelihood of getting a ticket, the size of the penalty, and the cost of putting the car in a lot. I decided it paid to take the risk and park on the street"
Gary Becker

"The most fundamental constraint is limited time"

B3CK3R

Gary Becker

In the case of Gary Becker, there was an individual economist who made a logical calculation that his best choice was to park illegally and hope for the best. If just one pioneering economist takes this unorthodox approach to parking, it is not a serious issue. But suppose everyone becomes inspired by this book to change their parking habits. Rather than arriving five minutes early to give ourselves time to park, we now all emulate Becker and arrive at the last possible minute, knowing it is logical to break rules and park illegally.

If everyone is willing to park illegally, the streets will become cluttered with cars parking in obscure areas, leading to a chaotic street. The local government may have to respond, probably by employing more parking wardens to increase the chance of catching offenders, and also by increasing the parking fine. Both these decisions will change the outcome until it is no longer profitable to park illegally. The first person to park illegally is probably all right. But, if everyone tries to do it, the rules of the game change. Therefore, if we are good citizens we will follow the rules and not exploit the probability of not getting caught. Do we want to encourage a society where we break the rules?

Diplomats usually have immunity from paying parking fines. Two economists, Raymond Fisman and Edward Miguel, found a correlation between illegal parking by diplomats and corruption in their home countries.

In other words, once you justify illegal parking it could be a slippery slope to breaking more rules. The 17th-century

Economic theory:

Rational choice theory suggests we should weigh up the costs and benefits of a decision and take the option with the highest utility.

English philosopher **Thomas Hobbes** (1588–1679) argued that without following accepted rules, human life would be "solitary, poor, nasty, brutish and short". Though he may not have specifically meant parking illegally, the point is that parking with consideration and respect for the laws is part of a social contract for a functioning society.

Doing the right thing

If you were to park illegally, the best place would probably be in an area reserved for the disabled. These spots are at least deemed suitable for parking – unlike parking spaces in front of fire hydrants or by corners (which are dangerous). Furthermore, the supply of disabled spots often outweighs demand. From a utilitarian perspective, it seems a waste for good parking spots to go unused. Perhaps you shouldn't take the last spot, but if several are available, why not risk it?

So would you want to park in a disabled spot, if there were a certain utilitarian logic to it? Probably not, or at least you wouldn't want to admit to it. The French sociologist **Pierre Bourdieu** (1930–2002) was critical of the *rational choice theory* proposed by Gary Becker and others, which stated that in making decisions, we will rationally choose those that will give us the greatest benefit. To Bourdieu, we make choices based not just on a sense of practical logic but also on social pressure from our peers and, as he put it, how we "feel for the game". We don't just base a decision on whether we will save the odd \$5 or arrive somewhere on time – we also base it on the feeling that we are doing the right thing. Gaining the approval of our peers can outweigh utilitarian calculations. If you park in a disabled spot, when you get out of the car, part of you will feel a little guilty; perhaps you will even feel compelled to fake a hobble. Just imagine your embarrassment if a work colleague spots you, and their "tut-tutting" that will accompany your walk of shame.

Weighing up the pros and cons

To come back to the question, can it make sense to park illegally? The answer is the usual economist fudge – it depends. If the illegal parking spot has no good reason for being illegal, then you may feel it is worth ignoring the rules of society and parking illegally. The important thing is to consider not just the cost of our parking ticket, but also the cost of driving around looking for a good space *and* how our decision will affect others.

A final way of looking at this problem is to change our view of parking tickets. Generally, we hate the idea of getting one. But why not see it as a gamble, where the odds are stacked in our favour? (At least it is better than gambling on horses.) We can win many times and save ourselves \$5. If we lose, we can console ourselves with the fact that we have contributed \$100 to our very deserving local government. If that doesn't make you happy, at least you will know you were following in the footsteps of a great Nobel Laureate economist!

Making a decision:

You may agree with the rational choice motivation of Gary Becker that if the personal benefits outweigh the personal costs, it is rational to park illegally and risk a fine. Or you may feel that, although it might make sense from a utilitarian perspective, it is more important to follow the rules and norms of society, even if it means arriving late.

What is the secret of happiness?

Jeremy Bentham • Alfred Marshall • Richard Thaler • Tibor Scitovsky • Dan Ariely
Bruno S Frey • Carl Menger • Betsey Stevenson

If you are seeking the meaning of life and how to find abiding happiness, consulting the so-called "dismal science" of economics may not be the most obvious starting point. Yet, despite its limitations, economics can offer a few insights for those trying to eke out a bit more happiness. These include mainstream economic theories of utility maximization and more modern evaluations of behavioural theory and "happiness economics".

The case to spend money

Some of the early economists, such as **Jeremy Bentham**, were utilitarians (*see page 15*) – they suggested that a basis for economics lay in the maximization of personal satisfaction/happiness. To Bentham, the goal of life was to maximize pleasures and minimize pain.

Early economists such as the highly influential English economist **Alfred Marshall** (1842–1924) took this idea and developed theories of consumer behaviour that assumed we sought to maximize our economic wellbeing on grounds of utility. Marshall and others developed *marginal substitution theory*, which states that we should consume goods up to the point where the *marginal utility* (satisfaction) is equal to the *marginal cost*. In a very simplified form, this means buy goods if they make you happy.

This *principle of marginal utility* can come in very handy for putting things in perspective. The American economist and Nobel Laureate **Richard Thaler** (b. 1945) writes about someone who subscribes to an annual gym membership, with a fixed cost of a $100 annual fee and the option of going to the gym whenever one wishes during that year.

Thaler was struck by a friend who after paying the fee injured his arm but continued to use the gym because he felt he ought to get his money's worth.

Here the consumer is making a mistake to worry about the $100 joining fee. Thaler rightly points out this is a *sunk cost* – once paid it is gone; you can't get it back. A secret of happiness is not to worry about sunk costs or, as your grandmother might say, "It's no use crying over spilled milk".

💵 Income	☺ Levels of happiness
0	3
10,000	6
20,000	7
30,000	7.5
40,000	7.5
100,000	7

How level of income might affect your level of happiness.

19

The only question to ask yourself is, what is the marginal utility of going to the gym? If you have an injured arm, it may be *negative utility* – you'd be better off staying at home. It's annoying not to be able to get value for money from your gym membership, but if you think like an economist, you won't get annoyed at the sunk costs, which are gone, and will only focus on the marginal utility of your next action.

The problem with utility maximization is that it can make life seem very…well, mathematical. If you're deciding whether to buy flowers for a loved one, do you want to be weighing up marginal utility against marginal cost? (If you do, don't mention it when giving the flowers.) Later economists have sought to be more thoughtful about the concept of utility.

The value of risk-taking
The Hungarian–American economist **Tibor Scitovsky** (1910–2002) in *The Joyless Economy* was critical of the standard economic link between welfare and consumption.

He claimed that higher consumption does not necessarily lead to higher satisfaction. In particular, he noted that there are two different types of positive experience – one is predictable pleasures such as eating cake and drinking beer, while the other is more unpredictable, risky experience that gives the potential for real progress, joy and lasting satisfaction. Scitovsky argued that real happiness does not come from Bentham's formula of maximizing pleasure and minimizing pain, but from taking risks, trying something different, learning what he called "skilled consumption".

Scitovsky mentioned a report stating that one-eighth of television viewers are almost continuously bored by TV. We watch it because it's easily available and is free at the point of use, but it gives a very shallow sense of pleasure and comfort. Scitovsky argued that greater happiness can be found from skilled consumption – learning to appreciate literature, culture and art. This requires more effort and risk, but it enables a real sense of joy rather than fleeting pleasure.

Passive happiness vs cultured happiness

> *"Why, then, do most of us attach so much importance to money income and the things money will buy?"*
> Tibor Scitovsky

Resisting temptation

At this juncture we might be thinking that Scitovsky has a point, but wondering why we end up making bad choices like watching television all night. We know it would be good to spend two hours catching up with work, but instead we waste the evening eating, drinking and watching TV, and then the next day we regret it.

Dan Ariely (b. 1967), an American behavioural economist, points out that humans are readily susceptible to a *present bias*. We eat chocolate because it maximizes the utility of the present moment, but we can spend the next few hours regretting our decision. Ariely suggests the key is to be aware of this present bias and try to remember the satisfaction we will get in the future by resisting temptation.

If you don't have the inner discipline of Gandhi, Ariely suggests making rules and nudges for yourself. Don't leave temptation around, and anticipate the happiness you'll get tomorrow from today's decision. Also, if you know you want to go on a diet, you have to make it easy for yourself – don't move next door to an ice cream store, but do fill your cupboards with vegetables.

Wealth and happiness

Evaluating the link between income and happiness welfare has become increasingly popular. Suppose we earn $70,000 a year; how hard should we push ourselves to earn more? The Swiss economist **Bruno S Frey** (b. 1941), in his 2010 book *Happiness – A Revolution in Economics*, claimed that the marginal increase in happiness from a higher income soon dissipated and just created a pressure in oneself to keep seeking a higher salary. Frey's investigations found that people were irrational in their behaviour – overestimating the utility of higher salaries in the future, and underestimating the happiness from non-marketable activities such as friendship and social interaction. Frey's work may sound as much of a New Age self-help guide as an economic text, but the implication is that there is value in ignoring the income maximization assumptions of some economists.

One reason we soon exhaust the happiness from extra income is the very strong *diminishing marginal utility* of extra income.

Economic theory:

Neoclassical theory (a model of economics that emphasizes the role of free markets and assumes that consumers and firms act rationally in seeking to maximize their utility/profit) begins with the assumption that greater production and consumption will bring more satisfaction and happiness.

This idea, developed in 1871 by the Austrian economist **Carl Menger** (1840–1921), observes that although the first unit may give a high utility, a second one gives much less. In practical terms, if you already own a car, illowill being able to buy a second one really make you happier? The logic of diminishing marginal returns suggests that rather than try to maximize the quantity of goods, you should seek a wider range of life experiences, such as travel and leisure.

In fact, there can even be negative happiness from extra income. In *The Challenge of Affluence*, the economic historian Avner Offer notes how rising incomes have created new problems, such as lack of exercise, obesity and stress (from the threat of losing your wealth). In other words, higher income potentially creates more problems than it solves.

However, if you're not convinced by a Buddhistic detachment with regard to income levels and you secretly aspire to own a fleet of BMWs, the American economist **Betsey Stevenson** (b. 1971), who has researched *happiness economics*, argues that there is, in fact, a strong link between income and happiness. She claims that wealthy people are the happiest people in society and happiness rises steadily with income.

The role of expectation

An interesting insight from Betsey Stevenson is that the absolute levels of self-reported happiness of women have declined since the 1970s – despite the period 1970–2000 being a period of rising job opportunities, a diminishing gender pay gap and a decline in the amount of housework done by women. To Stevenson it was a paradox. She suggested that one possible cause was differing expectations. In the 1970s women's expectations of careers were very low, but in the 21st century women have much greater hopes and expectations – therefore, when they fall short, there is greater unhappiness. This seems to suggest that if you want to be happy, it might be helpful to have low expectations – though, as Stevenson notes, it may also highlight the limitations of surveys asking people if they are happy or not.

Making a decision:

If our goal is to increase income and consume more goods, we will probably agree with the standard economic theory of Bentham and others. However, if, like Scitovsky, we feel that extra income would do little to make us happier, we should seek out the more challenging aspects of life and develop new interests that can give a satisfaction materialism never can.

How can I resolve disputes with neighbours?

Ronald Coase • Vilfredo Pareto • Jonathan Gruber • Richard Thaler
Daniel Kahneman • Ernst Fehr • Michael Sandel

We all have problems with neighbours but can economics offer us any practical solutions for dealing with noise, unkempt fences, boundary disputes and similar issues?

Fortunately, we have the work of a Nobel Laureate British economist, **Ronald Coase** (1920–2013), to help us here. His work is the basis of what became known as the *Coase theorem*. Coase cites an example of two neighbouring farmers: one grazing cattle, and the other growing crops. But there is a problem – the cattle are eating the crops, causing one farmer to face a financial loss.

Who should pay?

According to the Coase theorem, an efficient outcome would be for the cattle herder to pay compensation to the farmer whose crops are eaten – just as you'd expect. However, the theorem goes on to suggest that it doesn't actually matter who owns the property or who is the perceived wronged party – if the cattle herder owns the property rights for all the land, the crop farmer will be the one who pays the cattle herder to build fences and prevent his crops being damaged. According to the Coase theorem, this is because neighbours, when seeking a conflict resolution, will negotiate the terms of a financial contract until both are happy with the outcome.

To a non-economist this will be counterintuitive, so can the theory be of any help to us? Suppose your neighbour is responsible for maintaining a fence but it falls down, causing you to lose your privacy in your back garden. Your neighbour may claim he has no money to rebuild a fence. It is his right not to rebuild, but you have the cost of losing your seclusion. Let's suppose you are quite wealthy and you really value your privacy. Even though you are not responsible for the fence, you would be willing to pay the $500 to build a new one for your neighbour. Your neighbour is happy because you are paying the cost, and you are happy because you value privacy at more than $500.

That is the Coase theorem in action: property rights are defined, it doesn't matter that one party didn't want to build a fence, and the one who was really keen paid the cost. In other words, the Coase theorem suggests we shouldn't suffer in silence,

but should be willing to pay to resolve a problem/dispute – if we get a value greater than the cost to us.

In economic jargon, the Coase theorem suggests that, in the absence of transaction costs, if property rights are well defined, then market mechanisms will enable the two parties to solve their dispute and gain a *Pareto efficiency outcome*. The concept of Pareto efficiency, which was developed by the Italian economist **Vilfredo Pareto** (1848–1923), is a mutually beneficial agreement – one where everyone gains from a transaction (or at least no one loses out). And this Pareto efficiency is exactly what we are seeking in resolving neighbourly disputes.

Reality check

Nevertheless, some economists are critical of the Coase theorem's practicality. This includes Ronald Coase himself, who never shared the enthusiasm some other economists had for the theory in his name.

Also, as the American economist **Jonathan Gruber** (b. 1965) states, the theorem ignores the real world of social conventions and relationships. Suppose you live next door to a venue and on Saturday they play loud music, keeping you awake till 2am. This is annoying, so you would like to improve the situation. Therefore, you reach a deal that the venue can play loud music if they compensate you. At $50 per night-time hour, you are willing to put up with disrupted sleep. But would you feel happy asking a neighbour to pay you compensation?

Economic theory:

If there is a dispute between two parties, but clearly defined property rights, the two parties should be able to come to an efficient settlement.

Seeking justice

Also, suppose you overcome the awkwardness of bargaining with a neighbour, but the venue then says it is their property and they have a right to play music, so if you want a quiet night you have to compensate them $50. In theory, you might value a quiet night at $50, and according to the Coase theorem it doesn't matter who has initial property rights – but to you it does matter!

At this point, you may be thinking that you don't care about economic efficiency, so why should you have to pay a venue not to play loud music? The behavioural economist **Richard Thaler** argues that the Coase theorem is based on an unrealistic assumption about human nature. Humans do not see economic efficiency as the highest goal, he says – we place greater value on concepts like fairness.

From the perspective of a rational man, it really may be worth paying $50 to get a good night's sleep. However, we are not necessarily rational from this economic

> *"There is clear evidence that people dislike unfair offers and are willing to take a financial hit to punish those who make them"*
> Richard Thaler

perspective. The principle of paying someone to turn down the volume of their music seems unfair, and we refuse to engage in any economic transaction that seems to condone "bad behaviour".

A sense of entitlement

Another issue relates to the *endowment effect*. According to the psychologist **Daniel Kahneman** (b. 1934), we place more value on things we own because of the greater sense of attachment, and we feel aggrieved at any loss. As the venue owner, because it is our venue and our music we demand a really high price to stop our night's music. At the same time, as the neighbour, if we have been used to a quiet night's sleep we may want an "irrationally" high price to compensate for loss of sleep. In other words, our sense of endowment, or entitlement, prevents the theoretical market-based solution. Also, as Harvard professor of jurisprudence Duncan Kennedy states, the initial allocation of property rights does matter. If the venue has the property rights to loud music, we will have less wealth after the transaction!

Unfortunately, owing to transaction costs, the endowment effect and the social difficulties of bargaining, a neighbourhood dispute offering a market transaction is rarely a practical solution.

Reciprocal cooperation

However, behavioural economics could offer a common-sense approach to resolving disputes. One theory of economics suggests we are strong reciprocators, or, as the Austrian behavioural economist **Ernst Fehr** (b. 1956) puts it, people are *conditionally cooperative*. In other words, if someone does something bad, we tend to respond in kind, but if someone does us a favour we feel honour bound to return the favour. This knowledge can be very useful in dealing with neighbourhood disputes.

Suppose we are really annoyed by loud music – the temptation is to start an argument with the person making the noise. But, suppose we visit the venue and speak nicely, offering praise for their food and beer. Behavioural theory suggests that after you have been nice to the venue owner, they will be obliged to be nice to you, and as a result they may agree to reduce the music after midnight. Offering kind words and praising the quality of their beer costs nothing, but in return you get a much higher chance of a quiet night's sleep. According to the *economics of reciprocity*, this is better wisdom than taking out your wallet or threatening litigation. If you want something from a neighbour, see if there is some favour you can offer them instead of money.

Risky rewards

Another problem with the Coase theorem is the potentially corrupting influence of the markets. The American philosopher **Michael Sandel** (b. 1953), who has investigated the moral limits of markets, observes how

Sleep vs. profit

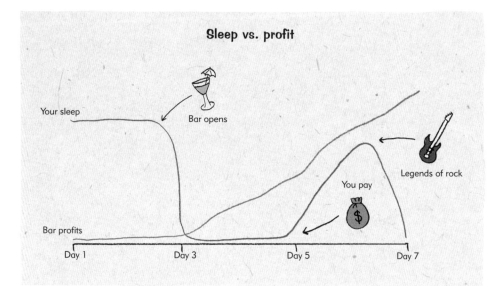

Your sleep

Bar opens

Bar profits

Legends of rock

You pay

Day 1   Day 3   Day 5   Day 7

financial incentives and contracts can diminish social cooperation. Suppose we do pay the venue next door $50 to reduce their loud music. The problem is that this influences their behaviour in the long run. The venue may think, "This is a good deal – I get paid $50 not to play music." Before you know it, Tuesday night is Legends of Rock Night and you are in a situation of needing to pay $50 to turn down the rock music on Tuesday night as well.

Sandel might ask whether you would pay your teenager to turn down his music for some quiet time. In one sense it would be economically efficient, but a parent could worry that paying a child to behave would send out all the wrong signals and encourage further bad behaviour in the long term.

If your neighbour is a large airport, seeking compensation may be advisable, but for small neighbourly disputes market-based solutions rarely offer much help.

Making a decision:

You may feel the Coase theorem offers a practical solution for resolving a dispute with a big company, but as regards neighbours you may agree with Sandel about the moral limits of markets. In this case, the conditional cooperation suggested by Fehr may offer a better way forward.

"Existing economics is a theoretical system which floats in the air and which bears little relation to what actually happens in the real world"

Ronald Coase

Is it better to gamble on the lottery or gamble by having no insurance?

Daniel Bernoulli • Milton Friedman • Leonard Savage • Daniel Kahneman
Amos Tversky • Richard Thaler

Individuals can display seemingly paradoxical behaviour. We gamble on buying a lottery ticket, which is an example of risk-loving behaviour. Yet in buying it the odds are stacked against us; gambling is a mug's game, as the law of averages dooms you to lose money. At the same time, we may exhibit risk-averse behaviour and buy insurance to reduce our risk of losing money. However, in the long run, buying insurance means we will receive less than we pay in. So how can we account for the paradox that we are risk-loving when the odds are against us, but we are risk-averse when taking out insurance which will, on average, make us worse off?

What does economic theory advise? In 1738, the Swiss mathematician **Daniel Bernoulli** (1700–82) made an early attempt to explain the choices of consumers under conditions of uncertain outcomes. This has become known as *expected value theory*. Bernoulli assumed that people take into account both potential outcomes and the probability of an event. For example, a 5% chance of winning $2,000 means that, on average, there is an expected value of $100.

This simple theory suggests that when making decisions we should weigh up the probability and the outcome, and create an expected value of the "game" – if it is played many times. However, while this may be appropriate for playing a game like poker, it is unrealistic to think games such as insuring your house are played an infinite number of times. You may play poker 100 times a year – the law of averages will give you that average payout. But death insurance is not a game we play many times. If you die early, that's it – you don't get to play an infinite number of times (reincarnation aside). If you're lucky with the first games of poker, over time your luck will run out. But, if you die early, that's game over. It's not much comfort being told your expected value was supposed to be a lifespan of 70 years.

> *"The same level of wealth, for example, may imply abject poverty for one person and great riches for another – depending on their current assets"*
> Daniel Kahneman and Amos Tversky

However, Bernoulli also noticed that some individuals were risk-averse and might prefer a guaranteed $80 rather than take the gamble with an expected value of $100. Bernoulli saw that additional money was worth more to a poor person than to a wealthy person. Therefore, a poor person might take a guaranteed $80 (risk-averse), whereas a wealthy person might choose to take a risk and try to win a gamble. This was an early awareness that different people can be risk-averse and risk-loving – though it didn't quite explain the paradox of someone being both risk-averse and risk-loving at the same time.

Variations with income level

In 1948, **Milton Friedman** and the American mathematician **Leonard Savage** (1917–71) developed a *utility function* that explains why we can display a different utility of money depending on our income levels. The utility of our first $10,000 is very high because this $10,000 is essential for the basic necessities of life. Increasing our income from $30,000 to $40,000 is nice, but the increase in satisfaction is of a smaller magnitude than the first $10,000. If our income falls from $40,000 to $30,000, we can still afford the basic necessities of life. This is why we want to insure against our house burning down. If we lost that it would be disastrous, but losing $300 a year on an insurance premium is absorbable.

The Friedman–Savage utility function was an attempt to explain how utility of money varied depending on income levels. But it was still criticized for being inadequate – for not explaining why rich people may like to gamble.

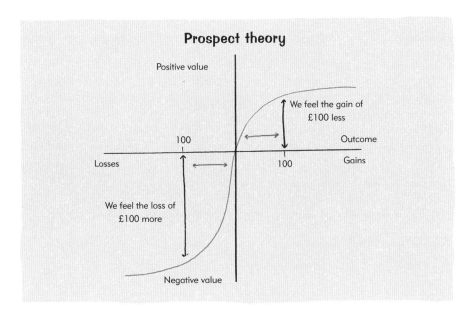

Prospect theory

Positive value

We feel the gain of £100 less

100

Outcome

Losses

100

Gains

We feel the loss of £100 more

Negative value

Relative prospects

Prospect theory (*see* page 29) is an example of *behavioural theory*, where economists try to take account of human psychology to explain why scientific methods may not be appropriate. Developed by the psychologists **Daniel Kahneman** and **Amos Tversky** (b. 1937–96) in 1979, prospect theory suggested that people make decisions from a relative starting point. At a current level of income we are more risk-averse to losing what we have. We are less attracted to gaining wealth compared with our attachment to what we have. If we own a house or car, we feel attachment to it. The thought of losing it fills us with apprehension. By contrast, the thought of gaining $300 a year in saved insurance premiums has relatively little attraction. This explains the logic of taking out insurance on expensive items. When deciding whether to insure, the law of expected value (and averages) does not seem the appropriate rule to consider.

Another aspect of prospect theory developed by Tversky and Kahneman is that

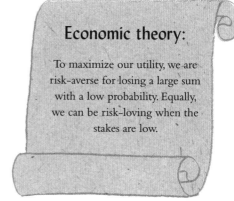

Economic theory:

To maximize our utility, we are risk-averse for losing a large sum with a low probability. Equally, we can be risk-loving when the stakes are low.

it takes into account how we may "frame" the issue in our mind. For example, we may struggle to evaluate probability. There may be a 0.0001% chance of our house burning down, but the mind focuses on the fact that it is possible. Similarly, there may be a one in ten million chance of winning the lottery, but the mind focuses on the fact that there is a chance of winning. It is hard to compute what one in ten million really means.

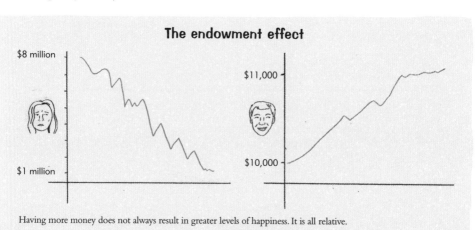

The endowment effect

Having more money does not always result in greater levels of happiness. It is all relative.

> *"...people valued things that were already part of their endowment more highly than things that could be part of their endowment, that were available but not yet owned"*
> Richard Thaler

This is why it may be rational to insure against a very small risk and take a gamble with a very limited chance of winning.

Who's happier?

Who do you think is happier, a poor person who gains an increase in wealth from $10,000 to $11,000 or a millionaire who has just seen their wealth fall from $8 million to $1 million? In theory, the person with $1 million should be happier, but individuals may not see it like that – the important thing is the relative change from what they had. The behavioural economist **Richard Thaler** called it the endowment effect (*see* page 25). It explains why we wish to insure what we have – we don't like the thought of losing it.

Insuring against a big risk

Suppose you buy a new car for $10,000. You reckon there is a very small, 5% chance of the car being stolen or crashed. But the insurance is expensive, at, say, $900 a year. If you don't insure, on average you will have a 5% chance of losing $10,000 – an expected loss of $500. But also, if you don't insure, you save the $900 a year premium, which is higher than the expected average loss of $500. If you feel like gambling, don't get insurance. But is this what economists would really advise?

The thought of losing $10,000 might prey on your mind all year, and you might perhaps focus not on the law of averages and expected utility theory, but on "Murphy's Law", which says that if anything can go wrong, it will. Worrying about losing everything could disturb your peace of mind, when, for the sake of $900, you could gain peace of mind. This loss of $900 you could afford, while the potential loss of $10,000 you could not. Sometimes it is rational to be risk-averse, when the potential loss is very high.

Making a decision:

Prospect theory and diminishing utility of income suggest that most people shouldn't gamble on avoiding insurance. However, if you're offered insurance on a new television, it may be different. In that case, it may be worth using expected utility theory because the potential loss is absorbable and this kind of insurance tends to be very profitable for the insurance company. If you feel like gambling, bet on your TV not breaking down.

Should I make an effort to turn off all the electric lights?

Gary Becker • Richard Thaler • John Maynard Keynes

Growing up, we almost certainly heard our parents reminding us to turn off the light, perhaps with the refrain, "Money doesn't grow on trees". These days, environmental factors give additional reasons to turn off electric lights – so can we really make an economic case to leave them on?

Does it add up?

Let us suppose electricity costs 15 cents per kilowatt-hour (kWh), and we have a bulb that uses 20 watts. If we leave this light on for 10 hours, it uses 200 watt-hours of energy, which is 0.2kWh, at a total cost of 3 cents. To turn this light off for one hour would save us less than a cent.

Suppose we are about to go out for two hours. At the front door we stop and think maybe we should spend five minutes going through the house checking the lights are off. Going through the house we find six lights on. Turning off six 20-watt lights for two hours saves us 120 watt-hours (0.12kWh) or 1.8 cents. But is saving 1.8 cents worth five minutes of our time?

As Benjamin Franklin advised, "Remember that time is money." Classical economists would agree – everything has an economic value. If we save 1.8 cents for every five minutes, it gives us a very low hourly wage of 22 cents per hour.

Making a rational choice

Gary Becker was a proponent of making greater use of rational choice theory (*see page 18*). The idea is that we should weigh up all the costs and benefits and make a logical decision from that.

If rushing out of the house saves time, and the marginal cost is only 1.8 cents – there is logic to not turning off lights. Furthermore, if you go out and leave all the lights on, perhaps there is a minor improvement in security. If six lights cost just 1.8 cents for two hours, it is much cheaper than employing a security guard at $60 an hour.

Paradoxical behaviour

But, if leaving on an electric light can be so cheap and is the rational option, why is

> "…*all human behaviour can be viewed as involving participants who maximize their utility from a stable set of preferences and accumulate an optimal amount of information and other inputs in a variety of markets*"
> Gary Becker

Spending 5 minutes
turning off lights
saves 1.8 cents

What is 5 minutes
of your time worth?

leaving on lights a big cause of family arguments? **Richard Thaler** developed a theory of consumer behaviour called *mental accounting*. He noted many paradoxes of consumer behaviour. For example, if our house falls in value by $10,000, we are probably not too affected. But something like seeing a light being left on can deeply affect our mental utility. This is why even very wealthy and generous people can struggle with the thought of leaving on a light unnecessarily. It is not so much the cost – 1.8 cents is nothing to a millionaire, but even a millionaire can suffer from the mental resistance to unnecessarily paying more to the electricity company.

We can go out for a meal and happily leave a $10 tip for the waitress, but when we get home our joy evaporates because we spent 1 cent on leaving an electric light on all evening. From the perspective of strict rational choice theory, it is illogical, but the insight of economists such as Thaler is that consumer behaviour is often illogical.

Keeping it in perspective

How should you react to someone leaving the light on? Becker might suggest that a useful life skill is to keep things in perspective. Here a bit of economic insight can help you enjoy life more. The next time a member of the family leaves the light on, remind yourself that the actual cost is relatively low. If it helps, use a bit of mental accounting in a positive way. Assume that every year you will lose $10 to lights being left on unnecessarily, but in return for that

If you're careful to turn lights off for 365 days, you may save yourself enough to buy a coffee.

lost $10 you can give yourself peace of mind and complete detachment about lights being on or off. To help, you could also see that $10 as a reasonable investment for improved security to deter burglars. The idea is to rationalize small losses.

So, what would the great British economist **John Maynard Keynes** (1883–1946) do in a situation like this? To be honest, we don't know. He never came up with a theory about turning electric light bulbs on and off; he was too busy writing theories on solving the Great Depression. Would Keynes have got annoyed about having to pay for a few light bulbs? Probably not. During the Great Depression, Keynes suggested paying people to dig holes in the ground and then fill them up. That doesn't seem like the kind of man who would have been too upset by the odd cent wasted on electricity.

However, is this what economics amounts to? A nit-picking analysis of whether it's worth the effort to turn the lights off? Consider this situation: if you visited your parents, would you explain rational choice theory to them and, since you prefer to leave lights on, offer to compensate them the 35 cents it would cost them to leave their lights on all evening? From a theoretical point of view, there is an economic logic to this. But, do people really behave like this? Of course not. It would be socially embarrassing.

Promoting harmony

When dealing with relationships, it can be a mistake to prioritize maximizing marginal utility (*see* page 19) and economic efficiency. Economists such as Paul Milgrom (b. 1948) note that many factors can influence our behaviour other than rational self-choice. Therefore, in real life, switching off lights is not just about the money, it is about caring for the wishes of others and signalling our

"Despite the attractions of the rational choice approach, its empirical failings in economics and psychology experiments have promoted an intense interest in new approaches"
Jonathan Levin and Paul Milgrom

care through small things like turning off lights. If your partner was brought up in the post-war austerity years, turning off lights is probably a deeply ingrained habit and we need to respect their preferences in our own choices. If you start bargaining with your parents to pay 35 cents per week, it contravenes all sense of promoting harmony in the family.

Stephen J Dubner, co-author of the best-selling *Freakonomics*, loves considering problems from the economic perspective of markets and incentives. He feels it is an anomaly that we tip waitresses but not flight attendants. In his logic, flight attendants deserve a tip as much as taxi drivers and waiters. On one flight he tried to tip a flight attendant, putting money in her hand. However, she was indignant – she refused the money and retorted, "I'm not a waitress". He never tried again.

This is a good example of economic theory clashing with social norms and expectations. Just because there is a certain logic in tipping

Economic theory:

Rational choice theory suggests we should put things in perspective and weigh up the costs and benefits of even small decisions.

flight attendants or leaving on electric lights doesn't mean it is advisable. Sometimes we have to put logic and marginal utility to one side and consider what counts to other people. If we take time to switch off the lights, our parents will think us a good son or daughter. If we try to bamboozle our partner with marginal utility theory, we may find ourselves paying for very expensive hotel rooms when we get kicked out!

Making a decision:

If it's your house, you might agree with Becker and rational choice theory that we shouldn't worry about always turning lights on and off, as the cost is minuscule. However, to maintain harmonious relationships with others, we may think more like Thaler and Levin – even if a financial cost/benefit analysis suggests something else.

Should I bother to recycle?

William Baumol • Thomas Kinnaman • Steven Landsburg • Mike Munger
Pieter van Beukering

In the past few decades, rates of recycling have increased as governments worry about the disposal of landfill waste and the depletion of natural resources. Despite the extra inconvenience, there is widespread public support for recycling. Yet some economists are not convinced. They argue that, taking into account all the costs and benefits involved, we might be better off just throwing garbage away. Can recycling be misguided, even though we feel it is a good thing to do?

The American economist and prolific author **William Baumol** (1922–2017) investigated the issue of external costs, or negative externalities (*see* page 13). Baumol suggested that if there are none, we should just leave recycling to the free market – if companies value waste for recycling, they will pay for it. But if there are external costs of landfill waste, it *may* be desirable to recycle – even if not profitable.

According to the World Bank, one external cost is greenhouse gas emissions – landfill waste accounts for almost 5% of the global total, and it is a growing problem. The World Bank estimates that the world's total municipal waste will rise from 1.3 billion tonnes in 2012 to 2.2 billion tonnes in 2025, and it is increasingly concentrated in urban areas, where there is diminishing availability of landfill sites.

The American economist Richard C Porter in his 2002 book *The Economics of Waste* argues that in determining the desirability of recycling, we need to weigh up all the social costs and social benefits. Recycling is beneficial because it reduces the costs of mining raw materials and the external cost of landfill sites, and recycled products can be sold back to industry. However, there are also social costs of recycling, including the cost of transportation, the recycling process itself and labour time for sorting waste (in terms of households and also staff at recycling depots). Therefore, although recycling may sound intrinsically good, its social usefulness is not guaranteed.

The situation is complicated by the fact that the price of recycled materials can vary.

Economic theory:

Recycling is desirable if the social benefit outweighs social cost. This includes not just the market price but external costs, such as pollution.

Ironically, the success of recycling programs in the US and Europe has increased supply and has driven down the price of recycled materials, making it less profitable than previously – recycling may be a victim of its own success. Some recycled plastics and glass have fallen so much in price that there have been occasions when recycled materials have eventually been put in landfill.

Looking at the state of recycling in 2002 and weighing up the social benefits and costs, Porter concluded that recycling probably did not make sense for most areas of the US, at least at that time.

It depends on the material

The American economist **Thomas Kinnaman** (b. 1965), who has researched the economics of solid waste and recycling, explains that the desirability of recycling can vary depending on the type of material. Some materials, such as tin, aluminium and steel, are very difficult and expensive to make from

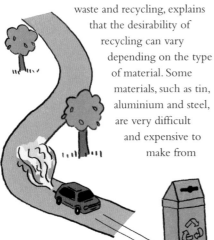

If you drive to a recycling bin to recycle plastic bottles, is it good for the environment?

virgin raw materials. Therefore, the price of recycled steel in particular is relatively high, and recycling these products tends to have a high rate of return. However, for other materials, like glass and plastic, the social costs of recycling are typically higher than the social benefits. Kinnaman points out that recycling is less environmentally friendly than we think. It takes energy to collect the waste, transport it to recycling facilities (which are often farther away than landfill sites), process it and then put it back in production.

A major motivation for recycling is concern over landfill sites. Kinnaman notes that no one wants to live next to a landfill site – if you live within about 3km (2 miles), your property may decline in value. Also there are concerns over methane emissions from landfill and the likelihood of running out of space, especially in regions with high population densities. Recycling helps to reduce the external costs of relying on landfill to deal with waste. However, Kinnaman observes that recycling is never straightforward; not only are the prices of recycled commodities volatile, but technology is changing. Modern landfills, at least in the developed world, are becoming much better at preventing methane emissions and leakages, and these sites can even be converted into generators of electricity from the waste gases.

Does recycling have an intrinsic value?

The Finnish economist Anni Huhtala argues that Finland's high recycling rate of 50%

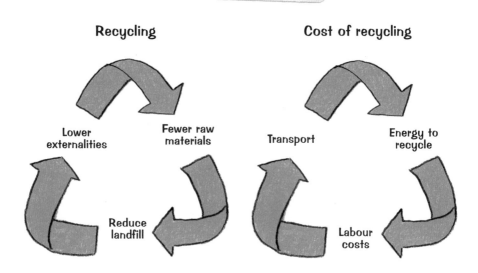

Recycling

Lower externalities → Fewer raw materials → Reduce landfill

Cost of recycling

Transport → Energy to recycle → Labour costs

is desirable from both an economic and an environmental perspective. However, in addition to the social costs and benefits of recycling, she is taking into account the environmental preferences of consumers. In other words, if consumers report getting satisfaction from recycling waste rather than putting it in landfill, then that is something we can add to the benefit of recycling. Thomas Kinnaman makes a similar observation, that one argument for recycling is that it may prove a gateway to more responsible, environmentally friendly consumer behaviour.

However, Kinnaman also observes that the other possibility is that recycling could be a convenient way to "offset" all our environmental sins. Putting plastic in the recycling box is cheaper and easier than making more substantial changes like cycling to work or reducing consumption. Therefore, recycling may make us feel good, but it is not as virtuous as we would like to think.

Steven Landsburg (b. 1954), an American libertarian economist (*see* page 12), is not impressed with the perceived "desirability" of recycling. In his book *The Armchair Economist*, he argues that recycling paper can lead to fewer trees and smaller forests because, if industry has more recycled paper, it doesn't need to plant trees. He makes the point that

> "Their real concern is with the ritual of recycling itself, not their consequences"
> Steven Landsburg

if there is a market value to recycling, it will happen, but if governments push us to recycle when the costs outweigh benefits, then it is a socially undesirable action. He also explains that it might be worth sacrificing some wilderness to landfill for the "luxury of not sorting your trash".

The time cost of recycling

The time involved in sorting recycling waste is an important consideration for many economists. Clark Wiseman argues that the labour hours involved in sorting waste are often underestimated or ignored, leading to an underestimation of the real costs of recycling; allowing for this pushes recycling beyond the economically efficient level. Rather than spend time in recycling materials, which have low value, the time could be more profitably used on productive environmental tasks such as picking up litter or researching ways to reduce the amount of packaging.

 Mike Munger (b. 1958), another American libertarian economist (*see* page 12), is also critical of universal recycling, arguing that recycling green glass has little value, and it is cheaper just to crush it and put it in landfill. Although sand is theoretically finite, it is not as limited and precious as time.

Recycling in the developing world

The Dutch environmental economist **Pieter van Beukering** (b. 1967) has investigated recycling and waste management across the world. He notes that there is a greater market for recycled products in the developing world, and this has led to a market for shifting waste from the US and Europe to countries such as China and India. This benefits Indian firms because they gain lower costs of paper, more jobs and economies of scale which make the recycling process more efficient. It is a controversial policy because it appears that the West is shifting its waste to poor countries, but van Beukering argues that if someone is paying for the waste, "you can bet someone is recycling". He suggests that our efforts at recycling could be beneficial for developing countries, even if they are not profitable for us.

Making a decision:

If you enjoy recycling, you are likely to agree with Anni Huhtala that we should recycle more. If you see no particular virtue in recycling, you may listen to Thomas Kinnaman and only bother to recycle metals where you are sure the social benefits outweigh the social costs.

How can I lose weight (through economics)?

Gary Becker • George Loewenstein • Richard Thaler • Daniel Kahneman
Thomas Schelling • Steven Levitt • Brian Wansink • Cass Sunstein

Across the world, obesity rates are rising. It seems that the only thing going up at a similar rate is our spending on the weight-loss industry. Despite fad diets coming and going, nothing seems to be able to halt and reverse our tendency to pile on the pounds. Yet some economists argue that everything could be solved by creating the right incentives, so how would the world of economics help us to slim down?

Economists of the rational choice school (*see* page 18), such as **Gary Becker,** argue that every choice is related to our perception of costs and benefits. The problem with obesity is that the benefits of eating are in the present moment, but the costs of gaining weight are something in the future. In economic parlance, we have a present bias (*see* page 21). Another problem is that the marginal weight gain of eating another peanut always feels very limited; there's no direct link between a slightly bigger portion and our weight gain. Therefore, our impulsive nature can overcome our good intentions.

George Loewenstein (b. 1955), an American behavioural economist, has come up with a *theory of hot–cold states*. In our "cold state" we would like to diet and lose weight. However, in a "hot state" (such as when walking into a restaurant with tempting aromas) we succumb to the environmental pressures and order more food than our diet plan allows. Any dieter will recognize this pattern of having our best plans go out of the window, but how can economics shift our compulsive tendencies?

Incentives and costs

Going back to the principles of Gary Becker, any problem, including eating too much, can be solved by changing the incentives and costs. So, if the cost of obesity is sufficiently high, we will choose a diet and lifestyle that avoids it. **Richard Thaler** writes about how two economists, John Romalis and Dean Karlan, came up with a rather drastic solution to losing weight; they signed a contract whereby they would each try to lose 30lb (13.6kg) over six months, and if either failed he would be liable to pay the other $10,000. This very high potential cost worked and provided the incentive to lose weight. To keep the weight off, they continued the financial incentive for the next four years.

Fortunately, you don't have to have to put $10,000 on the line to create the right incentive. On a smaller scale, **Daniel Kahneman** has written about an app that uses basic principles of behavioural economics to nudge individuals into making the right choices. The app allows users to commit to fining themselves for missing gym sessions, with the money

Pre-commitment strategy

If you fine yourself for gaining weight, it changes the rationale and it becomes easier to forsake the cake

going to other users who stick to their planned sessions. Kahneman notes that the thought of losing money – even a fairly small amount like $5 – can be an effective motivating tool because of the *loss-aversion* effect – we notice losses more than gains. These potential $5 fines are far more effective than paying in advance for membership of a gym or slimming club.

Strategies to put in place

The American economist **Thomas Schelling** (1921–2016) was awarded a Nobel Memorial Prize for his work on game-theory analysis. It was mostly related to conflict resolution, but Schelling argued that his work on game theory could also be used to overcome bad habits such as quitting smoking or going on a diet. He wrote from personal experience after having tried for 15 years to quit smoking. In theory, he saw a clear choice between smoking or quitting, but his brain kept coming up with a third option – "quit tomorrow" – which is the same principle as "I'll start the diet tomorrow".

Schelling looked at his own work on game theory and decided that "pre-commitment strategies" could help individuals choose the right option. He used the example of the Greek philosopher Xenophon, who suggested it was good to make an army fight next to a dangerous cliff – then the army had to fight bravely because there was no third option of fleeing battle. For dieting or quitting smoking, we just need to find a similar way to commit to the programme.

The problem is that many diet products and gym memberships give us this sense of a third option. As long as we buy diet products

> "If the person could make the final decision about that action at the earlier time, precluding a later change in mind, he would make a different choice from what he knows will be his choice on that later occasion"
>
> Thomas Schelling

or keep a gym membership, we feel we are making a token commitment to dieting – which prevents us doing what we really need to. In his essay "The Intimate Contest for Self-Command" Schelling suggests that pre-commitment strategies to improve self-control could include public resolutions, strict rules that allow no backsliding, and making it time-consuming to go and get the undesirable products.

One problem with dieting is that eating is so much more enjoyable than the alternative. If we smell freshly baked cookies it can quickly override our resolutions. But remember that the theory of rational choice states that we merely have to increase the cost of overeating and think like an economist. The American economist **Steven Levitt** (b. 1967) in his radio podcast "100 Ways to Fight Obesity" suggested carrying around a bottle of revolting smells. When tempted to overeat, we have an easily accessible mechanism to make food undesirable. This raises the effective cost of eating because it is no longer palatable. Levitt noted that health experts took no interest in his idea, even though it might be effective for so little cost.

> **Economic theory:**
> Changing the costs and benefits of eating can create the necessary incentives to stick to a diet and overcome our tendency to value present implications over future ones.

However, in addition to putting ourselves off food, we would need to consider the external cost of bad smells – putting our friends and family off their food, too. This drastic measure may find us eating alone, which may or may not be good for losing weight.

Be careful where you put the nuts

Another lesson we can learn from behavioural economics is how much our environment influences our choices. A 2006 study by the American economist **Brian Wansink** (b. 1960) researched observations

Open bowl – people eat. Closed bowl – easier to say no.

> *"When self-control problems and mindless choosing are combined, the result is a series of bad outcomes for real people"*
> Richard Thaler and Cass Sunstein

of *mindless choosing*. In an experiment that involved asking people to eat soup, one group had a bowl that automatically refilled from beneath the table. The group who ate from these bowls not only didn't notice but ate 73% more soup. Wansink also ran experiments asking people to make small behavioural changes to see if it helped them lose weight. The most effective changes were using smaller plates, not eating in front of the television and eating fruit before snacking.

Behavioural economics employs the terms *nudge* and *nudge theory* to describe the use of rewards and indirect suggestion to influence people's behaviour. Richard Thaler and **Cass Sunstein** (b. 1954), in their book *Nudge: Improving Decisions About Health, Wealth, and Happiness*, wrote about a trivial incident that had implications for behavioural economics. Inviting students around to dinner, he noted that many were eating lots of nuts from a bowl. Worried that they might spoil their appetites, he removed the bowl. Later that evening, many thanked him for doing so.

It is something we can all relate to. When food is easily available, we eat it because it is there.

Another example comes from Google's New York offices, where they used to put out M&Ms in open baskets but then tried putting them in bowls with lids. This change reduced the number of M&Ms consumed by three million a month. It's not rocket science but it shows how the *choice architecture* (the way goods are presented) of our kitchen and refrigerator can influence our eating habits. For dieters, this means making it easy to consume high-fibre, low-calorie food and difficult to eat foods that pile on the pounds.

If you're really desperate, the ultimate choice architecture would be to live in a country with significantly lower rates of obesity. While 27% of Americans are obese, in Japan it is just 2%, which suggests that something about American society, from size of portions to availability of fast food, creates the wrong nudges toward obesity, while in Japan the nudges are in the right direction.

Making a decision:

Economics offers a surprising array of suggestions. It's hard to ignore the importance of nudges and choice architecture mentioned by Thaler, Sunstein and Kahneman. However, removing temptation may not be enough, in which case we may follow Schelling's advice to find a way to prevent ourselves backsliding. Giving ourselves a financial penalty may be just the extra incentive we need.

What is the optimal number of children to have?

Steven Levitt • Robert E Weintraub • Gary Becker • H Gregg Lewis
Thomas Robert Malthus

The optimal size of a family may sound an odd topic for economists to consider, and when in the late 20th century the economist Gary Becker did start relating economics to the quantity and quality of children, it caused a storm of protest – how could we reduce family matters to mere economics? Yet, while being aware of the limitations of economic forces in matters of love and family, it would be a mistake to ignore them completely. Economics/finance is at least one compelling factor affecting the size of families.

An early form of economic theory was *mercantilism*. Mercantilists like Jean-Baptiste Colbert argued that the aim of economics was to accumulate gold and wealth.

The other way to help the economy was to have more children. More children resulted in a growing population and more resources for wealth accumulation. To a mercantilist, a high birth rate was the sign of a strong economy. Today, the mercantilist approach is unlikely to inspire many parents to have more children. Yet falling birth rates have led to a variety of new measures being pushed through to encourage large families, from countries such as South Korea, Denmark and Singapore, though with limited success. It seems that government ads have little influence over what we perceive as the ideal number of children.

Incentives to procreate

What about incentives for having children? In the 2005 book *Freakonomics*, the journalist Stephen Dubner and the economist **Steven Levitt** write, "Economists love incentives. The typical economist believes the world has not yet invented a problem that he cannot fix if given a free hand to design the proper incentives schemes." So perhaps we can relate financial incentives to our optimal family size.

After the fall of the Soviet Union, Russia's birth rate was at a record low. In 2007, the Russian government declared that 12 September would be National Day of Conception, and women who gave birth on that day had the chance to win refrigerators, money and cars. By 2011 the Russian birth rate had increased from 1.2 in 2000 to 1.7. In theory, material goods may give a financial incentive to have more children, and national campaigns may make larger families more attractive. Although many factors influence this question, government policy could affect our decisions on family size.

Financial pluses and minuses

Robert E Weintraub (1925–83), an economist who investigated birth rates and economic development, said that family size was related to basic economic factors – the proportion of the population in farming, infant mortality rates and income. For those in poor, rural societies, children become an economic asset to help on the farm; and for societies with zero state pension and health care, children become an insurance policy for old age. Weintraub noted that rising incomes in developing economies tend to lead to smaller families. With rising incomes, you don't need children to be an economic asset – you can afford for your child to be more of an economic liability.

While children in poor, agrarian societies contribute to family income, children in the developed world subtract from family finances through the costs of their education and upbringing. The costs of raising a child in the US have been estimated at anything from $200,000 to $1 million. We don't need an economist to tell us that children are very expensive, owing to the costs of college fees, maintenance, spending money and even the fact that we might have slower career paths because of time spent raising them.

The price of quality

Another factor to consider is what start in life you can afford to give your children. **Gary Becker** and the American economist **H Gregg Lewis** (1914–92) produced a paper in 1974 that examined the interaction between quantity and quality of children. They made the case that if you want to keep the "quality" of children the same, the *opportunity cost* of additional children will rise the more you have. (Opportunity cost is the next-best alternative you forgo.)

Talking about the "quality" of a child may seem deeply impersonal, but parents will be thinking about these issues, even if they use other terminology. They will feel that "quality" will depend on whether they, as parents, can give their children the best start in life, based on the family's financial resources and outgoings. In an increasingly competitive society, which values premium

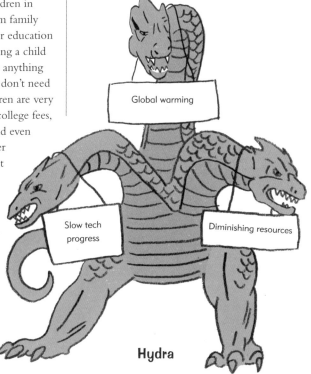

Global warming

Slow tech progress

Diminishing resources

Hydra

education, these costs can include school/college fees, perhaps extra tuition and extracurricular activities, possibly even moving house to live in the catchment area of a good school. As a result, parents may decide to have a smaller number of children so they can afford the "best" education.

In this model, Becker and Lewis basically say that it's not just about how many kids you want to have, but how much you want to spend on them to make sure they have the most advantages in life. Viewing the possibility of having extra children through this lens, it may only be the very wealthy families who can afford to have a higher number of offspring – reversing the trend in developing economies for higher income leading to fewer kids.

Weighing up cost vs utility

The marginal utility theory is important here. In essence, it asks, is the marginal utility of an extra child greater than the marginal cost? The marginal cost of another child is sleepless nights, greater anxiety and $233,610, according to a 2015 report by the US Department of Agriculture. The marginal utility is the intangible joy, love and happiness we get from a child. It is

Economic theory:

Marginal utility theory weighs up the cost of an extra child against the benefit. Given the potential costs and benefits, this theory is more relevant than ever.

true there are some things we can't put a price on, but economics provides a rough framework for deciding how many kids you want to have. Whether you want to bring up marginal choice theory with your partner is a different matter – some things are better left unsaid.

The worst nightmare of any parents would be to have another child and then after all that expense the child becomes a troublemaker. Fortunately, Gary Becker tells us not to worry – in his ground-breaking *rotten kid theorem* he argued that financial incentives would be sufficient to make even bad kids well behaved in order to maximize their family's, and therefore their own,

"The key feature in our analysis is that the shadow price of children with respect to their number (i.e., the cost of an additional child, holding their quality constant) is greater the higher their quality is"
Gary Becker and H Gregg Lewis

wealth. Becker argues that the selfish desire for money from their parents will encourage the child to be reasonably well behaved and maintain family harmony. The only caveat to this theory is that it requires parents to be wealthy and have the capacity to leave an inheritance. With no inheritance to speak of, our rotten kids may not even bother to look after us in old age.

Will the population outstrip the food supply?

Generally speaking, when having children we don't consider the wider implications for society and the future. But, it would be a shame to examine this question of population growth without a nod to the English economist **Thomas Robert Malthus** (1766–1834) – the man who was indirectly responsible for giving economics the label "the dismal science".

Malthus was incredibly pessimistic about the chances of survival for our world. He assumed that the global population was increasing at a faster rate than its ability to grow food. To Malthus the only logical consequence was famine, death and the end of civilization as we know it. If you take the theories of Malthus at face value, it definitely makes you think twice before having several children. Fortunately, the prophecies of Malthus have been rebutted on many occasions. The world population expands at an exponential rate, yet we still have food surpluses; such is technological progress.

However, a bit like the multi-headed hydra, as often as Malthus is rebutted, his theories reappear in another form; this time is different, we are told. Technological progress can't keep giving us exponential growth in agricultural production. The environment is close to breaking point. Global warming will make the planet less hospitable. We could definitely take this as a case for having fewer children. On the other hand, the more children we have, the greater the probability we will give birth to the next Einstein or Newton – someone who will be able to solve the world's problems and find a solution to all these people living on earth.

Making a decision:

If we agree with Becker and Lewis and we aspire to give children the best education and the best start in life, it may require a calculation to have fewer children, unless we are very rich. However, despite these economic considerations, we may reject completely the importance of finance and economics and follow our heart rather than our wallet.

The consumer

Page 50: If I enjoy drinking beer, how much should I drink?

Page 54: Can I trust a second-hand car salesman?

Page 58: How do we best manage common resources?

Page 63: Should I pay to go to the front of the line?

Page 67: How much should we give
to charity?

Page 71: Should I give a gift or money
for a Christmas present?

Page 76: Should I favour buying local
goods?

Page 80: How can I get a good deal
when shopping?

Chapter 2

If I enjoy drinking beer, how much should I drink?

Jeremy Bentham • John Stuart Mill • William Stanley Jevons • Alfred Marshall
Carl Menger • John Richard Hicks • John Maynard Keynes • Irving Fisher

If drinking beer gives you joy, how do you work out the optimal amount of beer to drink? If something is good to do, does this mean it is good to do to excess? How could a brilliant economist like Keynes make such an elementary mistake as to drink insufficient champagne?

An important concept in economics is marginal utility (*see* page 19), which refers to how much enjoyment you get from the last unit of a good consumed. It derives from the philosophy of utilitarianism (*see* page 15), which was proposed and popularized by the English philosophers **Jeremy Bentham** and **John Stuart Mill** (1806–73) in the 19th century. This philosophy suggested that the best course of action was to maximize your happiness and that of society. If drinking beer gave you pleasure, the utilitarian philosophers would say to drink without guilt. Utilitarianism sought to challenge more rules-based morality, and the approach appealed to economists trying to codify consumer behaviour.

Bentham was a philosopher, social reformer, legal reformer and advocate of rights for women, gays and animals – so it is not surprising that he also turned his hand to a bit of economics. In particular, Bentham was an early pioneer in the evaluation of consumer choice. The *principle of utility* appears quite a lot in economics, so it is useful to consider what it actually means. Bentham argued that in evaluating the utility of a decision we should rank our pleasures and pains according to their "dimensions", such as the certainty of happiness resulting from it, whether the happiness will be short-lived, how the decision would affect our future happiness, and so on.

A heavy beer drinker may instinctively like the apparent hedonism of utilitarianism, but since Bentham asks us to consider the duration of happiness and the future consequences, he is suggesting we should be careful when assessing how much utility we really get from drinking several glasses of beer. Short-term pleasure is only one aspect of utility. If we suffer a hangover the next morning, this needs to be taken into consideration in evaluating our choice.

One more beer

After early utilitarianism, the economist **William Stanley Jevons** – and, later, **Alfred Marshall** – developed the concept of marginal utility. This emphasized the utility of an extra glass. In other words, when deciding how much to drink, you don't evaluate simply how much you like beer – but how much you would like one extra glass at this particular time. Jevons also noted that a rational consumer should compare the

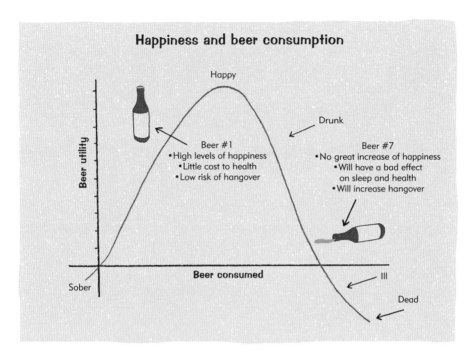

Happiness and beer consumption

Happy

Beer utility

Sober

Beer #1
• High levels of happiness
• Little cost to health
• Low risk of hangover

Drunk

Beer #7
• No great increase of happiness
• Will have a bad effect on sleep and health
• Will increase hangover

Beer consumed

Ill

Dead

marginal utility of the beer with the price. Just because you like beer doesn't mean the utility from a seventh glass is greater than the cost.

In 1871, **Carl Menger** continued the development of the theory of marginal utility with an observation of *diminishing marginal returns*. This concept is particularly relevant to the optimal level of beer drinking. If you are thirsty, the first glass of beer will give a high utility, with little cost to your health and head. However, if you have already drunk six glasses of beer, what will the marginal utility of the seventh be? It is at this level of consumption that an extra beer will give you

declining happiness. It is that seventh glass that will exacerbate tomorrow's hangover and leave you feeling wretched for the next day. While the first beer may give you a lot of satisfaction (positive utility), there is a possibility that the seventh could make you feel ill (negative utility).

Some goods, such as water consumption throughout your life, exhibit slower degrees of diminishing marginal utility. Few people start to get negative utility from drinking water. But with something like drinking beer or eating cake, we have to be aware that extra units can rapidly give diminishing marginal returns.

> *"My only regret is that I have not drunk more champagne in my life"*
> John Maynard Keynes

In order to compare changes in the utility of something, economists use a standard unit of measurement known as the *util*. Now at this point you may be thinking it is all very well for economists to come up with a concept like utils – and, indeed, when you are purchasing items like beer it is very difficult to assign figures to arbitrary amounts of "util". In fact, the more you drink, the more difficult it may become to measure utility. Later economists felt that the concept of giving a numerical value (known as *cardinal utility*) to consumption isn't relevant to the real world.

The influential British economist **John Richard Hicks** (1904–89) argued that what happens is that we give a simpler order of preference. Which do I prefer? Seven beers (costing $21) and a hangover? Or three beers (costing $9) and no hangover? Hicks argued that this ordering of preferences is a more realistic portrayal of life. Perhaps when we are young, we prefer trying the first outcome. But, over time, our willingness to turn up to work with a headache declines, and we start to prefer greater moderation.

Beers	Total utility	Marginal utility
	0	0
	10	10
	15	5
	18	3

How rational is our judgment?

If **John Maynard Keynes** regretted not drinking more champagne, a contemporary of Keynes – the great American economist **Irving Fisher** (1867–1947) – took completely the opposite view. Fisher, who came from a strict Protestant family, was an ardent supporter of Prohibition in the US. He believed that if you liked to drink beer, you were mistaken and the government should change your decision. It is interesting that Fisher attacked the utilitarianism of Jevons, arguing that individuals often mistook desire for satisfaction.

"The additional benefit which a person derives from a given increase of his stock of a thing diminishes with every increase in the stock that he already has"
Alfred Marshall

Fisher was making a case that alcohol is an example of a *demerit good* – a good where consumers undervalue, or ignore, the costs of consuming it, and the consumption of which can harm others in society – effects known as negative externalities (*see* page 13). However, what constitutes a demerit good is only a matter of personal opinion (known as a normative statement or value judgment). Our subjective perception can also affect our view of our alcohol intake because of our tendency to *optimism bias*. This concept in behavioural economics states that we tend to overestimate the likelihood of positive things happening to us personally (such as the benefits of drinking) and underestimate the chances of negative things (like a hangover) happening to us.

The concepts of a demerit good and optimism bias present a challenge to neoclassical economics (*see* page 21). According to mainstream economics, consumers can evaluate the utility of something – or at least make rational preferences. But neoclassical economists

Economic theory:

Marginal utility theory states that we will maximize our welfare by consuming a quantity of goods that enables us to gain the most satisfaction given our limited budget.

like Fisher believe that individuals can't be trusted to make the correct choices, and that there should be regulation to change their behaviour.

So should we listen to Keynes or to Fisher? Instinctively, most people would like to think that they are perfectly capable of calculating the marginal utility of drinking more beer. However, we might have to admit that such knowledge has often been gained through occasions where we did significantly underestimate its diminishing marginal utility.

Making a decision:

You may agree with Keynes and Bentham: drink and be merry! But, don't forget about diminishing marginal returns – just because you like beer doesn't mean you will enjoy the seventh beer of the day. Or you may feel, like Fisher, that beer is much overrated and there are more illuminating pleasures to be had, such as studying economics.

Can I trust a second-hand car salesman?

George Akerlof • Thomas Gresham • Michael Spence • Alex Tabarrok • Tyler Cowen

A car is one of the most expensive items we will purchase, but people often approach buying a used car with a degree of trepidation. Are we correct to distrust second-hand car salesmen or should we put our faith in market forces?

The souring effect of lemons

In 1970, the American economist **George Akerlof** (b. 1940) wrote the influential paper "The Market for Lemons: Quality Uncertainty and the Market Mechanism". Now considered a ground-breaking work, it eventually gained Akerlof a Nobel Memorial Prize in 2001. (Interestingly, back in 1970 it was rejected by three economic journals, one of which said, "If this is correct, economics would be different.")

The paper touched on the problem of whether we should trust a used-car salesman. Akerlof observed that in certain transactions there is *information asymmetry*. This is a technical way of saying the used-car salesman knows the quality of the car, but the consumer doesn't. (It suggests there is some truth in the joke, "What's

Potential peach but risky

the difference between a used-car salesman and an insurance salesmen? The used-car salesman knows when he's lying.") For the consumer, information asymmetry means we don't know whether we are buying a "lemon" (poor-quality car) or a "peach" (high-quality car).

We are faced with a dilemma if the second-hand dealer is asking a high price (suitable for a high-quality car) that we are reluctant to buy. This is because we fear that, although the car may look well polished, we have no real way of knowing whether it is ready to break down as soon as we drive off in it. Because people don't trust used-car salesmen, it is difficult for them to sell genuine "peaches" at a high price. Akerlof argued that in second-hand markets, prices will tend to fall toward a mid-price between peaches and lemons. The used-car salesman can't get a fair price for genuinely good cars, but the consumer still risks ending up with a real lemon – at a high price. The implication of this scenario is that we are correct to be suspicious of second-hand car dealers.

Akerlof argued that another problem is that because the price of second-hand cars is adversely affected by this problem of lemons, someone with a genuinely good

Guaranteed lemon but cheap

second-hand car will be reluctant to put it on the market because they know it won't reach a fair price. Therefore, the second-hand market attracts lemons, while peaches are held back. This, too, should make us more reluctant to buy a second-hand car because we should expect a preponderance of low-quality cars. Akerlof called this *adverse selection*.

Back in the 16th century, the English merchant **Thomas Gresham** (*c.*1519–1579) observed that "bad money drives out good money", and three centuries later this became known as *Gresham's Law*. Gresham was referring to exchange rates, but here we can apply the principle to a related idea, that "bad cars drive good cars from the market". According to Akerlof, honest car dealers are at a disadvantage. They don't try to sell lemons at inflated prices, but they do suffer from the actions of unscrupulous dealers who sell lemons and thereby reduce market prices.

According to Akerlof, the implication is that if you are trying to buy a second-hand car, you're more likely to stumble across a rogue dealer than an honest one.

Ways around the problem

However, not all economists would caution such pessimism about the second-hand car market. Israel Kirzner's 1976 article "Knowing about Knowledge: A Subjectivist View of the Role of Information" suggests that entrepreneurs and consumers find ways around this problem of potential lemons. One simple solution is for used-car salesmen to offer warranties on their automobiles.

The libertarian economist (*see* page 12) William L Anderson continues this theme by suggesting that market imperfections are part of the market process. He notes that when buying a second-hand car, people could pay an expert to check the car for defects. If you are spending $10,000 on a new car, paying a car expert $100 to check the car helps to increase the efficiency of the transaction. If you don't have a car-mechanic friend, you could bluff and pretend your friend is an expert. The fear of being exposed may be enough – how would the car dealer know that your companion is not a car expert? This would be your own information asymmetry!

"The cost of dishonesty…lies not only in the amount by which the purchaser is cheated; the cost also must include the loss incurred from driving legitimate business out of existence"
George Akerlof

Furthermore, Akerlof himself conjectured that the market for lemons could be mitigated to a certain extent. He noted that the presence of warranties and reputations could offset some of the information asymmetries. In recent years, there has been a growth in the number of large-scale second-hand dealers – "car supermarkets" specializing in high-end second-hand cars. The size and volume of these national dealers provide strong incentives to avoid selling lemons. Selling a few lemons at high prices may earn a quick buck, but the reputational costs are bad business, and as consumers we know this.

The American economist **Michael Spence** (b. 1943), who won the Nobel Memorial Prize in 2001 with Akerlof, investigated the use of *signalling* – a way for dealers to signal that their cars are not lemons. If a firm invests in advertising and large premises,

Economic theory:
Information asymmetry means that the consumer may be at a disadvantage in buying a second-hand car. It could mean we end up with a poor-quality car and are right to be suspicious of second-hand car dealers.

I'M PAYING
FOR ADVERTISING

SO YOU CAN
TRUST ME

these sunk costs (*see* page 19) convey that the firm can afford to advertise and is planning to stay around for a long time, which implies that you can probably trust the dealer.

Furthermore, in an era of internet reviews and mobile tracking, it is easier for dissatisfied customers to leave feedback and for potential buyers to see more information about goods they are buying and whom they are buying them from. Economists **Alex Tabarrok** (b. 1966) and **Tyler Cowen** (b. 1962), co-authors of the economics blog *Marginal Revolution*, support this view in their 2015 article "The End of Asymmetric Information". They argue that modern technology has enabled buyers and sellers to find ways to overcome many informational asymmetries, and that though these may have existed in the pre-internet age of 1970, they do not in our modern digital world.

In 2002 the economists Winand Emons and George Sheldon investigated the market for used cars in Basel-City, Switzerland,

> *"Asymmetric information is no longer a plausible description of the used car market and, as a result, we should not be surprised that these markets are thriving, whether in terms of volume, diversity of product, or their ability to deliver a reliable purchase at a reasonable price"*
> Alex Tabarrok and Tyler Cowen

where the cars were subject to mandatory vehicle safety inspections. The study found that buying a second-hand car privately increased the chance of its having defects – thus confirming Akerlof's theories. However, they also noted that second-hand cars bought from dealers led to a reduced chance of defects. In other words they were more reliable than the average used car. The implication is that if you want to buy one, get it from a large second-hand distributor who look like they are planning to stay around for a long time, but give a wide birth to private dealers.

At this point you might be thinking that you didn't need an economist to tell you that a large dealer is safer than a shady character selling a used car from a bar. And, according to the logic of free markets, it doesn't matter where you buy – the market has already assigned a fair value; the fact that private sales are more risky and quality is likely to be lower is reflected in the price differentials. But can't we have our cake and eat it? Can't we buy a peach at a low price, missing out the car dealer's profit and the risk premium?

Kate Raworth, author of *Doughnut Economics* (2017), suggests that a problem with neoclassical economics (*see* page 21) is the assumption that everyone acts out of selfish interest. According to Raworth, this ignores the reality of human nature which includes reciprocity, social responsibility and reputational effects. In other words, why do we have to assume someone selling a second-hand car is out to rip us off? If we get to know the seller or if it is someone in our locality, social pressures may encourage them to be honest. This approach may enable us to get the best of both worlds – low price, good car and adding to levels of local social trust.

Making a decision:

If we accept Akerlof's theory, then buying cars from private sellers will be more risky (though, equally, they are cheaper). However, we may agree with Cowen that in this internet age, buying from dealers now gives greater reliability in terms of quality and so we are right to trust large dealers.

How do we best manage common resources?

William Forster Lloyd • Elinor Ostrom • Hernando de Soto
Milton Friedman • Garrett Hardin • Michael Heller

If there is a shared resource with no obvious ownership, how do we best go about managing and looking after this resource? Is it possible to cooperate with others and prevent mismanagement? Or is the only solution to divide up the resource and gain piecemeal private ownership?

In 1833 the British economist **William Forster Lloyd** suggested that a common area of meadowland, which has public rights of use, could easily be subject to overgrazing, a concept called the Tragedy of the Commons (*see* page 15). Lloyd assumed that individuals are rational utility maximizers (*see* page 10) – they try to get the most value for the least cost, which is a basic assumption of mainstream economic theory. However, if you have 100 villagers maximizing their private utility, they may ignore the *socially efficient level* (optimal level of production for society), leading to overgrazing of the common land.

If people know that the land is being overgrazed, they may cut back on its use to protect the resource. However, the problem is that there is an incentive to *free-ride* on other people's moderation. Even if we use the resource in a reasonable amount, it may not be enough – because others free-ride on our moderation and the resource is lost anyway. If we see a common resource degraded in this way, we may feel the necessity for government regulation, to place limits on its use. For example, depleted fishing stocks have required government legislation to prevent overfishing.

As well as overuse, common resources can suffer from neglect. In modern life we may not be too concerned about overgrazed meadows, but we do get annoyed when the shared office kitchen is always a mess. This is the same free-rider problem – people don't clean up, hoping someone else will do it!

Spontaneous cooperation

The American political economist **Elinor Ostrom** (1933–2012), who was the first women to win the Nobel Memorial Prize in Economics (in 2009), argues that the theoretical case of the Tragedy of the Commons rarely matches reality. In practice, local communities find effective ways to manage shared resources. In her influential work *Governing the Commons* (1990), Ostrom cited many examples of local communities who did this, without government intervention or private ownership. She mentions, for example, many Alpine communities in Switzerland and Germany who effectively self-regulate common grazing areas and have learned over centuries which resources are best managed collectively and which through private ownership. Far from free-riding on others,

Field split in 4

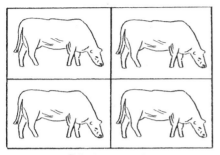

Private property

No private property

Commons overgrazing

Private property prevents the Tragedy of the Commons.

the sense of community, local pride and self-regulation encourage people to voluntarily look after the shared resources.

Therefore, according to Ostrom, it is definitely possible to create local frameworks that reward responsible behaviour and discourage and penalize irresponsible behaviour. Going back to shared kitchens, the student kitchen area may be a mess, but by the time we graduate and work in an office, we are more likely to develop rules, such as taking turns to keep the kitchen clean.

In her book *Doughnut Economics* Kate Raworth offers a critical look at conventional economics, arguing that economic theory too often assumes people to be rational self-servers, when the reality can be different. The point is that, with common areas, there could easily be overconsumption and market failure in theory, but in practice there are much stronger bonds and a sense of social responsibility, which can be encouraged within the right environment.

If you are inspired by the logic of local collective action, you might be interested in the "eight design principles" for *Common Pool Resource (CPR)* institutions suggested by Ostrom. These emphasize the importance of creating self-organized systems, which rely on internal trust, effective monitoring by those affected and a provision of common resources appropriate to local conditions.

Ostrom's work challenges the dominant view of economics which places emphasis on self-interest theory and not enough on how human beings can behave in the setting of

> *"…a maxim I call Ostrom's Law: A resource arrangement that works in practice can work in theory"*
> Lee Anne Fennell

"Humans have a more complex motivational structure and more capability to solve social dilemmas than posited in earlier rational-choice theory"

Elinor Ostrom

local communities. In evaluating the impact of Ostrom, Lee Anne Fennell, an American law professor and specialist in land use, notes how Ostrom looked at reality first and then created theories from that.

The power of private property

While local self-regulation can work in some cases, the Peruvian economist **Hernando de Soto** (or Hernando de Soto Polar; b. 1941) takes a very different approach. In his work *The Mystery of Capital* he argues that a lack of clearly defined property rights is a stumbling block for developing economies becoming richer – and in particular a challenge for the poorest section of society who feel no sense of legal empowerment. De Soto explains that when there is a lack of trust in property rights, physical assets become "dead capital", a term he coined for a dwelling for which the property rights are not clearly defined, meaning it cannot be used as collateral for a loan. This makes it much harder to give people the confidence to invest in business. For example, without private ownership of housing, utility companies are reluctant to invest in infrastructure because it is harder to get people to pay.

> ### Economic theory:
> Managing common resources shared by many people can lead to overconsumption or neglect because of a lack of clearly defined property rights.

De Soto argues that, far from encouraging a vague sense of local resource sharing, we should seek to define property rights – even if it means splitting up resources into smaller units. De Soto claims it is only when people have property rights that they feel a real sense of responsibility and a share in the fortunes of the economy. His ideas have been embraced by free market economists, such as **Milton Friedman,** who emphasize minimal government intervention apart from the protection of private property. However, it is worth bearing in mind that de Soto doesn't just support the status quo but also believes the key is extending property rights to those who currently live in poverty with no current sense of ownership. From a practical point of view, it may mean lobbying government to give property rights for your local housing, resources and amenities.

From the perspective of solving a messy shared kitchen, de Soto's philosophy may involve limiting everyone to using only a

PLEASE TIDY AFTER USE

> *"Ruin is the destination toward which all men rush, each pursuing his own best interest in a society that believes in the freedom of the commons. Freedom in a commons brings ruin to all"*
> Garrett Hardin

single plate and single cup – so everyone is forced to wash up their own property and there is no option to free-ride on others' clean plates.

Overuse and abuse

To ecologists, unregulated commons protected by private property or relying on local cooperation may still lead to overconsumption. In 1968, American ecologist **Garrett Hardin** (1915–2003) argued that, without proper regulation, many common resources could be overused. For example, in cases of logging, cutting down trees may provide short-term payoffs, but it also changes the long-term ecological balance of nature, threatening sustainability. To Hardin, it shows that, for sustainability, relying on self-regulation may be insufficient. Instead government regulation, which can consider the longer-term impact, is necessary – for example, strict (and unpopular) fishing quotas have successfully protected fish stocks in the North Sea.

A final thought is from **Michael Heller** (b. 1962), an American professor of property rights, whose book *Gridlock Economy* suggests that if there is too much separate private ownership of one resource, it can lead to gridlock and prevent optimal use. Heller gives the example of patent trolls who buy up patents, not to create helpful products, but to sue any company who uses something similar. Going back to our meadow, if it were split among several private owners, one awkward owner might be in a position to make life difficult for all the others wanting to pass through to the water supply, to say nothing of legal costs that can arise over disputes about correct access.

Making a decision:

If you agree with Ostrom's optimistic views on self-regulation, you should work with neighbours and members of your local community to pursue responsible consumption and use. However, if you think this is unlikely you may prefer the philosophy of de Soto and seek private property rights. Alternatively, for long-term environmental sustainability, you may agree with Hardin and feel that the only option is for government regulation.

Should I pay to go to the front of the line?

Gary Becker • Michael Sandel • Adam Smith • Alvin Roth

Recently, there has been rapid growth in companies allowing consumers to pay to go to the front of the line. You can pay for priority boarding at airports or pay to queue-jump in amusement parks. There is even a growing market for paying people to stand in line for you. From an economic perspective, this is usually considered efficient, and if we have the money, it could save us considerable time. However, is this a trend we should be encouraging?

The economics of queue-jumping is another example of rational choice theory (*see* page 18) in action. An economist such as **Gary Becker** would state that we can treat paying to go to the head of the line like a commodity, not dissimilar to buying a business class ticket. If the perceived benefit of reducing waiting time is greater than the marginal cost (*see* page 19) of paying, then this is a desirable transaction. Furthermore, if we allow people the freedom to buy goods, buying a shorter wait in a line is just a different application of *price theory* (that prices are set by the interaction of supply and demand).

Paying someone to stand in line for you

Michael Sandel writes about the long lines of people waiting to see a US Congressional hearing. Increasingly, those wanting to go to a hearing pay a company $36–$60 an hour to get someone to stand in line for them. It is a transaction that increases economic welfare. You save time, someone gains employment (the place-holder typically earns $10–$15 an hour) and no one loses out. After all, **Adam Smith** encouraged *division of labour* (where workers are given specialized jobs within production processes) within an economy. Why should a brain surgeon spend three hours standing in line, when a homeless man could have gainful employment and do the unskilled job of standing there for him?

However, although paying to avoid standing in line has an economic logic, Sandel is concerned that paying to jump the queue to see an elected representative could be seen as creating a two-tier democracy. If you can afford this, you effectively get a preferential say in the democratic system. Those with less income lose the chance to lobby Congress. Paying to cut in line may be acceptable for inconsequential goods like leisure, but should democracy be more open to those who can afford to pay?

A popular example of queue-jumping is buying premium tickets to go to the head of the line in amusement parks. It definitely benefits some parties – the amusement parks increase their revenue, and those who can afford it get shorter waiting times. But Felix

Oberholzer-Gee, a professor of business administration, warns that pushing in front of people who have been standing in line for half an hour may lead to visible resentment from those who can't afford it and have to stand there longer because of the VIP guests. You get a shorter wait, but there is a cost – someone gets a longer wait. Sandel and Oberholzer-Gee ask whether we would feel comfortable about this.

If we feel uneasy about cutting in line, we have to include this guilt in our rational decision-making progress. (On the other hand, you may get great pleasure from pushing in front of people!)

How everyone can benefit if you pay to go to the front

If, like the author Stephen Dubner, you support the principle of paying to cut in line, you may wish to point out another advantage of this approach. If someone pays to queue-jump, there can be benefits for everyone in the line. Effectively, paying to jump a queue is a form of price discrimination – the firm has found a way to charge higher prices

> ## Economic theory:
> According to marginal utility theory, if a consumer gains a benefit from paying a premium to have a quicker service, then it is rational and efficient to pay to jump the queue.

to wealthy customers for a similar good. Priority boarding by budget airlines creates higher revenue, which, in turn, makes lower ticket prices possible for everyone else. Although those who pay to go to the front of the line at security won't get to their final destination any quicker than ordinary passengers, they have helped to reduce the cost of the other passengers' tickets. The message is, don't feel guilty – you're helping to subsidize cheaper tickets for others.

Most people probably don't feel too resentful of priority boarding, but what

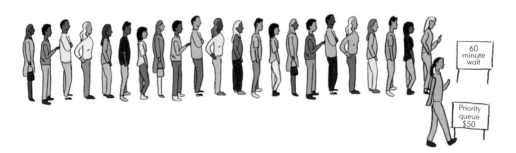

60 minute wait

Priority queue $50

> *"The ethic of the queue, 'First come, first served,' has an egalitarian appeal. It bids us to ignore privilege, power and deep pockets – at least for certain purposes"*
> Michael Sandel

about health care? Should we pay to jump the queue to get treatment ahead of others? In the case of, say, kidney transplants, given the shortage of kidney donors is it right to prioritize utility theory (*see* page 10) over morality in this particular market? The American economist and Nobel Memorial Prize-winner **Alvin Roth** (b. 1951) calls it an example of a *repugnant transaction* – something you might like to do but others feel is morally wrong. Whatever our attitudes on the morality of the issue, paying for kidney donation would increase supply and enable us to jump the queue, and people offering a (spare) kidney would gain monetary compensation. Roth admits that it takes economic principles into a grey area of morality, but if your child were dying from kidney failure, how much would you be willing to pay to jump the queue?

The Canadian psychiatrist Lloyd Maybaum proposed that if wealthy people want to jump the queue for healthcare surgery, they could be made to pay five times the social cost of the operation. In that way, they would gain quicker surgery while raising money for those also waiting in the queue. In effect it becomes a type of *Robin Hood tax* (taking money from the rich to help the poor). We may not like the idea of a rich person jumping the queue, but what if it meant more resources for health care and quicker treatment for everyone else?

The joys of standing in line

Most economists would view the need to stand in line as an inefficient allocation of resources. However, the behavioural economist Ayelet Fishbach questions this view. He says that queues themselves can have an *intrinsic value*. He works on ways to encourage consumers to value self-control, patience and the long-term pursuit of the goal. Rather than seeing a queue as a deadweight welfare loss (*see* page 71) to be avoided at all costs, we can view it as part

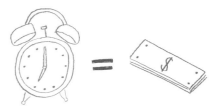

of civic society – waiting patiently in line, perhaps chatting to strangers, gives a shared social experience that is more valuable than trying to bribe your way to the front. This is a utility maximizing strategy (a strategy for finding a situation that will give you the greatest personal satisfaction).

What happens if you offer money to jump a queue?

Oberholzer-Gee conducted an experiment trying exactly that, in a cafeteria. As expected, the more money offered, the more likely people were willing to allow the queue-jumping. However, after letting the person in, they rarely accepted the money. Oberholzer-Gee felt that jumping the queue was not a normal transaction but a gift exchange – people let the queue-jumpers in because they recognized they were desperate. The other thing he noted was that people wouldn't allow a repeat queue-jumping by the same person at any price. He felt that people saw a certain ethic in queue-jumping that couldn't be bought and sold like a

transaction. In other words, there are some queues that it may be acceptable to jump, but be careful about flashing money around to push in front of people in your local bar – you may end up with a black eye.

Undermining civic virtue

Michael Sandel is worried that if it becomes common to pay to jump queues, it could subtly change social norms. In a country like Britain or Canada, waiting in line is seen as being of positive social value (it has even been mentioned in the British citizenship test). But if the market for jumping queues becomes widely accepted, where will it end? If I pay for priority boarding, why should I stand at the back of a bus queue? It could create a society where the poorest spend longer in traffic jams and lines. Material inequality is one thing, but always being at the back of the queue may create a much greater sense of resentment.

Making a decision:

If you value the time saved more than the cost, economists like Gary Becker would argue this is an efficient use of your money. However, you may agree with Sandel and Oberholzer-Gee that there are some queues where it may be better just to stand in line and enjoy the sense of encouraging civic virtue.

How much should we give to charity?

Frank P Ramsey • Jeffrey Sachs • Simeon Djankov • Peter Bauer • Jagdish Bhagwati
Steven Landsburg • James Andreoni • Gary Becker • John Maynard Keynes

Economics is often seen as a subject that promotes rational self-interest, so can it offer any insights into the concept of altruistic giving? Is there such a thing as pure altruism or does everything, even charity, come down to maximizing our own self-interest?

The idea of *perfect altruism* was first suggested in 1928 by the British economist, mathematician and philosopher **Frank P Ramsey** (1903–30). It implies we should give to charities if we feel the project has a genuine need of our money. For example, if there is a need for clean water supplies, we should give money because we value having that public good provided for in our society. If we are truly altruistic, we will not attempt to free-ride (*see* page 58) on the charitable donations of others.

Jeffrey Sachs (b. 1954) is an American development economist who has argued that increasing the rate of charitable giving is essential for the eradication of poverty in the developing world. According to Sachs, many countries in Sub-Saharan Africa lack the basic resources and capital even to get to the bottom rung of economic development. He claims that aid can play a pivotal role in helping the poorest countries to break through the cycle of poverty and pave the way for states in which their economic

development can become self-sustaining. Sachs campaigns for people and governments in the developed world to increase their donations to charitable projects in Africa. As a simple example, distributing free insecticide-treated mosquito nets could help reduce the $12 billion cost of malaria in Africa. Charity is a powerful way to increase net global welfare.

The aid curse

However, not all economists share this enthusiasm for giving aid, and they point to a concept known as the *aid curse*. The economist **Simeon Djankov** (b. 1970), Bulgaria's former deputy prime minister and minister of finance, argues that generous foreign aid can lead to poor governance, damage institutions and lead to non-productive rent-seeking. For example, in Burkina Faso during 1985–89, aid accounted for two-thirds of the government budget. Such a large proportion can lead to aid dependency and make the government reluctant to collect enough taxes to become

"[Foreign aid is] an excellent method for transferring money from poor people in rich countries to rich people in poor countries"
Peter Bauer

self-sufficient. Djankov argues that foreign aid can actually undermine democracy, as corrupt politicians seek to control and manage the aid flows. A similar argument was put forward by **Peter Bauer** (1915–2002), a Hungarian-born British economist widely known for his opposition to state-controlled foreign aid to developing economies.

The India-born American economist **Jagdish Bhagwati** (b. 1934) is sceptical about aid. He makes the point that increased charitable aid can lead to a decline in private sector savings. In other words, when recipient countries get used to receiving foreign aid it reduces their incentive to increase domestic saving. In fact, aid can create a problem of *moral hazard* (people taking riskier action knowing they will get some kind of protection) – if you save less, you become eligible for more aid and charity, which encourages less saving.

Bhagwati argues that the key to economic development is the promotion of free trade. For example, he notes that the biggest poverty alleviation in modern history has been in China and India. In these countries, he says, it was economic reforms and not foreign aid that helped millions of people to escape the poverty of a stagnant economy. It suggests that buying manufactured goods might be as effective as the donation of aid.

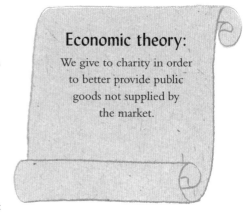

Economic theory:
We give to charity in order to better provide public goods not supplied by the market.

Whether you support giving aid to Africa or to cancer research, **Steven Landsburg** argues that you should choose the best charity and then give all your money to that one single cause. He claims that if you think one charity is the best, it makes no sense to split your charitable donation with a second-best charity. Suppose you feel that the biggest problem in the world is starvation, then it would be logical to give money only to a charity like Care International until the problem of extreme poverty is solved. He argues that no matter how much you give to Care, it won't make a serious dent in the problem of starvation, but you will still be helping individuals and so you should keep giving as much as you can.

> *"Apparent charitable behaviour can also be motivated by a desire to avoid scorn of others or to receive social acclaim"*
> Gary Becker

> *"If you care only about the recipients (as opposed to caring, say, about how many accolades you receive), then you will bullet all your contributions on a single charity"*
> Steven Landsburg

The joy of giving

At this point, you might be thinking that only an economist could come up with such a counterintuitive idea. But, if you instinctively dislike Landsburg's suggestion, the American economist **James Andreoni** (b. 1959) proposes a more nuanced view of why we give to charity. He argues that the reasons we donate are complex, but a significant factor is the personal satisfaction or warm glow we get from giving. We don't donate just to make sure clean water is provided in Malawi – we give money to charity because we get satisfaction from the actual act of giving. In this sense, if we give $1,000 to one charity, we get one opportunity to feel good. If we give $100

to ten charities, we get ten chances to feel good and we don't have to worry about trying to work out which is the best charity.

Gary Becker puts it in slightly different terms. He argues that our charitable behaviour can be motivated by a desire to receive social acclaim or avoid social scorn – hence charitable foundations often publish a list of donors. Evidence suggests that we give more money to charity when there is someone around to notice our giving. A study by Craig Landry et al. found that if an attractive female was soliciting for charity, it led to an improvement in charitable giving of 50–135%. From a purely altruistic model, it is irrational to give small amounts

Double benefit of charity

Reduce poverty

Feel good about yourself

to anyone who asks – especially to charities we may not know much about. However, if we get satisfaction from our giving being acknowledged, then from the perspective of rational choice theory (*see* page 18), this joy of appreciation is an important part of the equation. Whether we care about the charity or not, it may be rational to donate $5 to a work colleague for his sponsored cycle ride – it is a small price to pay for appearing generous and good-hearted!

Another study by Landry et al. found that the most successful way to raise money for charity was through selling lottery tickets. To the sociologist Marcel Mauus, this is entirely predictable, as he sees this "gift exchange" as an intrinsic part of society. In other words, we like to give to charities where we get something in return – be it very small like a ribbon or sticker or a chance to win a prize. Gary Becker would say that there is nothing wrong in giving for these reasons – the charity benefits from the money, and you benefit from feeling good.

Should we give to charity at all?

What if you don't feel like giving to charity at all? Is there any way out? Steven Landsburg offers the thought-provoking view that misers are unknowingly very generous. Landsburg's argument is that if a miser has the capacity to deplete the earth's resources but chooses not to, it means there are more resources for everyone else. It is the logic that if you earn a dollar but don't spend it, the world is better off because you produced a good you didn't consume. Landsburg argues that "while philanthropy serves a favoured few, the miser spreads his largess far and wide".

John Maynard Keynes would definitely not agree with this counterintuitive approach. He would argue that hoarding of wealth can lead to unused savings, which results in lower growth and wasted resources. If we all became misers tomorrow, living standards would plummet. And, of course, being miserly does nothing to overcome the market failure of underprovided public goods.

Making a decision:

If we value pure altruism we may take the lead of Landsburg and give all our money to the one charity we feel will make the biggest improvement in social welfare. However, you may agree with Andreoni that part of the attraction of giving to charity is the warm glow you feel after giving to a worth cause. This impure altruism actually has a double benefit – the charity benefits and we get utility from the act of giving.

Should I give a gift or money for a Christmas present?

Alfred Marshall • Joel Waldfogel • E F Schumacher • Milton Friedman
Richard Thaler • Ryan Bourne

Buying presents at Christmas can be stressful, as it's both expensive and difficult to know what to choose. However, help may be at hand. According to one strand of economic thinking, gift-buying at Christmas is an inefficient allocation of resources – far better, goes the theory, just to give cash and save all the bother. Could this way of thinking catch on?

Back in the 19th century, **Alfred Marshall** outlined the principle of marginal utility and marginal cost (*see* page 19). It stated that, assuming consumers are rational and well-informed, they should buy goods where the satisfaction from an extra unit is greater than or equal to the marginal cost. The problem with this mainstream economic theory of utility maximization (*see* page 10) is that, at Christmas, it seems we have a system guaranteed to cause inefficiency and market failure – with the utility of gifts much less than the cost.

Unappreciated presents

According to the American economist **Joel Waldfogel** (b. 1962), author of *Scroogenomics*, surveys of students found that they valued Christmas gifts up to 33% less than the actual cost. Thus the practice of giving gifts leads to what is known as a *deadweight welfare loss* (in which money spent is greater than utility gained, leading to an inefficient allocation of resources). For example, if the gift cost $15, then on average we will feel it is has a value of $10. Waldfogel claims that means that, for the US 2012 holiday season, the total deadweight welfare loss of gifts was $4–$13 billion. Furthermore, environmentalists such as the economist and statistician **E F Schumacher** (1911–77) might add to these unwanted Christmas presents the environmental costs of using more resources and creating more pollution.

But, what does it mean that Christmas gives a deadweight welfare loss? In examining the practice of giving gifts, Waldfogel noted there is information asymmetry (*see* page 54) between the buyers of gifts and the receivers. What this means is

> *"An important feature of gift-giving is that consumption choices are made by someone other than the final consumer"*
> Joel Waldfogel

that when Aunty Jane buys us a Christmas present, she only has partial information about what we would like. Therefore, she makes a guess and we end up with a bright red sweater. This cost her $20 – but gives almost zero utility to ourselves. In fact, it may even be negative utility because we have to feign how happy we are to receive it and then, out of obligation, keep it in our drawer for a few years – giving us an unwanted cost of storage.

Milton Friedman came to a similar conclusion about the inefficiency of buying gifts in his talk "Four Ways to Spend Money".

Christmas cash and spreadsheets

According to Waldfogel and Friedman, a far more efficient transaction would be for Aunty Jane to give us $20 in cash or gift tokens so we could decide how to spend it ourselves. In fact, if we take this idea to its logical conclusion, rather than swapping $20 gift vouchers we could do Christmas by spreadsheet, with everyone noting in a profit-and-loss account how much they want to give.

Oscar Wilde famously said that a cynic (or perhaps economist) is "a man who knows the price of everything and the value of nothing". In fact, if we wished to be cynical, we could make the assumption that the people who want to abolish Christmas are Scrooge and mainstream economic theorists.

The point of gift-giving

When economic theory seems to challenge common sense, it is helpful to look beyond the subject. For example, essayist Lewis Hyde, in his 1983 book *The Gift: How the Creative Spirit Transforms the World*, takes a view that is in contrast to the whole basis of economics. He argues that the point of gifts is not to create an efficient market settlement, but to unsettle the balance and make parties unequal.

The anthropologist and sociologist Marcel Mauss, in *The Gift: Forms and Functions of Exchange in Archaic Societies*, notes many examples of reciprocal gift-giving being important for creating social bonds, trust and community – even if from a strictly

"You can spend your own money on yourself. When you do that, why then you really watch out what you're doing, and you try to get the most for your money. Then you can spend your own money on somebody else. For example, I buy a birthday present for someone. Well, then I'm not so careful about the content of the present, but I'm very careful about the cost"
Milton and Rose Friedman

economic point of view it is inefficient. Gift-giving creates a new sense of trust, commitment and obligation between parties.

However, some economists argue that we don't need anthropologists to defend the desirability of Christmas. They claim that the analysis by Mauss just shows the limits or misapplication of marginal utility theory (*see* page 35).

Reasons for pleasure

Richard Thaler developed the concepts of *acquisition utility* and *transaction utility*. Acquisition utility is the utility we get from using a particular object. Suppose you give your mother a new vacuum cleaner for Christmas. It has a high acquisitional utility because it cleans the house. If you give her an ornament, it has a less obvious acquisitional utility, but it has sentimental value – there is an emotional satisfaction purely because of

the person who gave it. However, there is more to life than acquisition utility.

According to Thaler, an additional element is transaction utility, the satisfaction we get from the act of buying or receiving a good. For example, if we get a 25% discount, this gives us transaction utility because we like a bargain. Similarly, if we receive a gift from someone we care about, we get transaction utility simply because we like receiving things from loved ones.

In a way, this does not contradict traditional utility theory but is merely a wider understanding of what utility actually is.

The economist Diego Zuluaga argues that one element of gift-giving is the idea of a signal. Buying and wrapping a present is a signal that we care. We may not want actually to say "I love you" to our mother (unless we really have to) but we don't mind buying some expensive perfume, wrapping

Your present from Nan	Transaction utility	Acquisition utility	Positive externalities
SALE 50% off	+ Nan gets discount	+ Jumper is warm	+ Nan likes giving gifts
	+ You care about Nan	− You won't wear it	+ Sister enjoys you pretending to like it
$60 → $30		− You have to store it	+ Family enjoys sharing gifts

There is more to giving and receiving gifts than costs and utility values.

it up and hoping she likes it. Of course, she probably wouldn't have chosen the fragrance we bought, but she is happy we made the effort. As the old adage says, it's the thought that counts. Would our mother really prefer a $20 note?

Unexpected benefits

Another feature of giving gifts is the issue of *positive externalities* (benefits to other people). When our Aunty Jane gives us that bright red jumper, our sister gets joy in seeing us unwrap it. Our sister knows we will hate it, so she can enjoy watching us pretending to like it. So, even if the utility we personally get is low, other people in our family get pleasure from the shared experience of opening presents.

Unwrapping presents is certainly more fun than the Christmas spreadsheet or the swapping of gift tokens. Furthermore, the economist Kristian Niemietz posits

"Most of us are not Scrooges. We like to spend money on nice things around Christmas. But we also like to moan about and sneer at other people doing the same. Why?"
Kristian Niemietz

that there is considerable utility in the "surprise factor" of receiving gifts – a factor that will tend to be higher for people who have pretty much all they want anyway.

Ryan Bourne (b. 1987), from the Institute of Economic Affairs (a British think-tank), points out that Waldfogel omitted to measure the utility of the person giving the gift. It is not unreasonable to assume that people get as much (if not more) joy from giving as from receiving. Even if we are not keen on Aunty Jane's Christmas jumper, she presumably got joy from shopping, buying and giving it, which outweighs my personal deadweight welfare loss.

Bourne also says that, although gifts often disappoint, occasionally we get a present we would never think of buying ourselves. Thus, there is a lottery element in receiving presents – we start with low expectations, but occasionally we get lucky and receive a higher utility than we could get from buying things ourselves.

Economic theory:

Because of information asymmetries, it is more efficient to give relatives cash for Christmas presents. This avoids deadweight welfare loss from unwanted presents.

Finally, Bourne notes that gift-giving is not a black-and-white issue – perhaps there are ways to improve the process, such as cash transfers for extended family or wish lists for close family members. In this way we can have the best of both worlds – the joy of giving and receiving presents, but without having to worry about getting a suitable present for our niece.

Making a decision:

If you have many embarrassing Christmas sweaters in your drawer, you may agree with Friedman and Waldfogel that you'd be better off with cash. However, you may take the side of Bourne and Zuluaga, who say that Christmas presents give a type of joy that cash efficiency never can.

Should I favour buying local goods?

Adam Smith • Friedrich Hayek • Russ Roberts • Steven Landsburg
E F Schumacher • Tim Worstall

Governments and local businesses often exhort us to buy local –
appealing to our sense of national and regional identity. The logic may
seem common sense but, fortunately or unfortunately, economists have
convincing arguments that it really is efficient to import tomatoes from
the other side of the world.

In 2017, US President Donald Trump signed
the order "Buy American, Hire American".
He claimed that buying domestic goods helps
protect domestic jobs, reduces the trade deficit
and improves living standards. Did he have
a point? How can it make sense to import
potatoes from across the world, when your
neighbour can produce them down the road?

Self-interest isn't so bad

An ardent supporter of *free trade* (international
trade free from restrictions such as tariffs or
quotas), **Adam Smith** warned back in the
18th century about the dangers of relying on
domestic producers. He argued against the
"interested sophistry" of domestic industry
which would encourage consumers to pay
higher prices for their inferior domestic
goods. According to Smith, a consumer
is misguided if he thinks purchasing only
domestic goods is doing his country a favour.

Suppose we have two goods: a car produced
in Australia and a Japanese import. Good
Australians might feel they should favour
the car manufactured by their countrymen,
but their patriotic purchase also has a cost
to the economy. They will spend a higher
percentage of their wage on the domestically
produced good, leaving less to spend
on other domestically produced goods.
Australian car producers may benefit, but the
more efficient Australian beer manufacturers
will lose out because Australian car-buyers
waste money on expensive local products.
Buying local can end up being a transfer
from more efficient producers to less
efficient ones.

For those who are still not convinced, the
20th-century economist **Friedrich Hayek**
gives us free rein to pursue our self-interest,
rather than feeling we should be patriotic.

> *"If a foreign country can supply us with a commodity
> cheaper than we ourselves can make it, better buy it of them
> with some part of the produce of our own industry"*
> Adam Smith

> *"But don't pretend that it creates wealth when I am getting less value for my money than I could get elsewhere. It doesn't"*
> Russ Roberts

Helpful knock-on effects

However, not everyone agrees that buying the cheapest imports from global companies is necessarily the best solution. Michael Shuman, an expert on community economics, argues that there is an alternative to globalization and cheap imports. He calls it *Local Ownership Import Substituting (LOIS)*. If people buy local, he claims, more wealth will stay in a community owing to the knock-on effects of local supply chains.

Similarly, David Boyle, a researcher from the New Economics Foundation, a British think-tank, found that buying local helps more money stay in the local economy through a multiplier effect. If you buy from your farmer neighbour, he can spend more in your community's restaurants, helping more wealth to stay in the local economy.

The "buy local" fallacy

Other economists dismiss this as a fallacy. The economics commentator **Russ Roberts** (b. 1954) argues that if we favour more expensive local producers, we diminish competition, limit resources, limit gains from specialization, encourage inefficient producers and fail to increase wealth. He claims that we may feel it is a charitable thing to do, but our local community will not benefit.

Also, Roberts asks, where do we stop? We may start out preferring national products, then move on to regional products, then choose products from just our town – does that mean we should just buy from friends and family? If we follow this argument to its logical conclusion, we will be self-sufficient and keep the money in our community but we also will be very poor. As the 20th-century economist Fritz Machlup said, "The logical consequence of protectionist measures is the left arm should not buy from the right arm."

Many campaigns to buy local focus on food. But **Steven Landsburg** is critical of this "locavore" (buy food locally) movement. He argues that if tomatoes are cheaper to import from Spain, then that is preferable to buying tomatoes from local producers. To Landsburg, the market price is the best indicator of social cost. For example, growing tomatoes in Norway may require extra electric heat and light, so in that case it would be more efficient (and less polluting) to import them from sunny Spain.

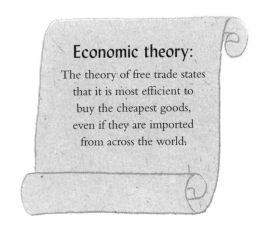

Economic theory:

The theory of free trade states that it is most efficient to buy the cheapest goods, even if they are imported from across the world.

77

> *"The advice I would give is: If you have the courage
> to do so, don't feel patriotic in monetary matters.
> Choose the money which helps you best"*
> Friedrich Hayek

The bigger picture

Some criticize Landsburg for under-estimating the external costs (*see* page 13) of importing food. In 1992, the food-policy adviser Tim Lang coined the term *food miles* to describe the distance food is transported, from producer to consumer. The problem is that high food miles (especially when the food is transported by air) contribute to carbon dioxide emissions and have significant environmental costs, such as pollution and global warming. Lang argues that these external costs make buying locally produced food a rational way to increase economic welfare and diminish environmental costs.

From a more philosophical perspective, the 20th-century economist **E F Schumacher**, author of *Small is Beautiful*, argued that traditional economics is based on a false goal of persistent economic growth, greater efficiency and the idea that "big is better". Schumacher took a totally different perspective, suggesting that economics should emphasize local communities and sustainable practices more than the holy grail of maximizing economic growth. In his model of economics, buying local can be desirable, even if does not maximize GDP (*Gross Domestic Product*, which is the national income of a country).

When it comes to the crunch

However, from a more practical perspective, **Tim Worstall** (b. 1963), of the British think-tank the Adam Smith Institute, notes that although people may say they prefer to buy from domestic producers, their actions often contract this. It may sound appealing to buy patriotically, but when we go to the supermarket we buy the cheapest, or as Worstall says, "money speaks louder than economic patriotism".

Also, a problem with favouring domestic producers is that, if taken to its logical conclusion, doing so would severely limit choice. Buying local strawberries seems attractive in season, but if you live in Alaska or Mongolia the idea of buying only local food becomes increasingly unattractive. Pierre Desrochers and Hiroko Shimizu write in *The Locavore's Dilemma: In Praise of the 10,000-mile Diet*, "If modern-day

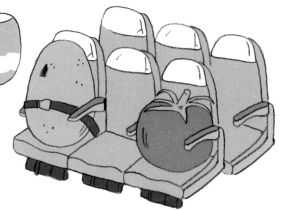

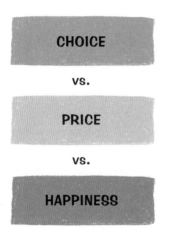

CHOICE

vs.

PRICE

vs.

HAPPINESS

of globalization? I want to support local farmers and I would get happiness from doing it. In this case, you can simply fall back on the marginal utility theories of David Ricardo and William Stanley Jevons (*see* page 10). If you get happiness and satisfaction from buying goods from local producers, then that is a rational economic logic to use. The perceived utility to others in your community should not be discounted. In the 2017 article "The Welfare Economics of 'Buy Local'", Jason Winfree and Philip Watson argue that if consumers perceive that buying local has significant positive externalities (*see* page 74), then buying local could increase *net economic welfare* (when the utility gained for society is greater than the cost – even if prices are higher).

activists were to cling to any consistent notion of 'local' food, a truly 'made in the USA' agricultural diet would be limited to turkeys, some farmed native fish and shellfish, sunflowers, blueberries, cranberries, Jerusalem artichokes, and some varieties of squash."

At this point, you might secretly be thinking, who cares what economists say about free trade and the efficiency

Given a choice between importing food from the other side of the globe or buying food from a farmer down the road, there is a good case to buy locally. However, would we want to take this approach to the extreme and aim for self-sufficiency? If we did, we would have to accept significantly less choice and lower living standards.

Making a decision:

In reality, we all make use of free trade, buying food and goods from across the world, as Adam Smith would have encouraged. Yet although we buy imports from abroad, we may prefer a partial compromise, in which we also make an effort to buy local products where we feel it is practical.

How can I get a good deal when shopping?

Tim Harford • Robert H Frank • Richard Thaler • Cass Sunstein
Vernon L Smith • Dan Ariely • Daniel Kahneman

When we go shopping how do we know whether we are really getting a good deal or are just losing out to clever marketing strategies? Behavioural economics offers insights into both the psychology of consumers and how firms manage to extract profits from unsuspecting shoppers. Being armed with this knowledge gives us an insight into our own shopping habits and how we can get a better deal.

Price discrimination is one way that firms try to get us to pay more. The British economist and journalist **Tim Harford** (b. 1973) refers to it as price targeting, and it involves setting higher prices for those customers who are willing and able to pay them. To some extent, we can't avoid this practice. If we need to travel by rail at peak time to get to work, we have no option but to pay higher fares. However, even shopping in our local supermarket can involve price discrimination we may not notice.

Harford notes that pre-packed vegetables that supermarkets sell can be up to ten times more expensive than vegetables sold loose, by weight. To some extent, this can be explained by a difference in cost, but mostly it is a case of supermarkets taking advantage of the fact that some customers are less price-sensitive

and buy packed vegetables for convenience, ignoring the price. Consumers who are willing to take a little time to pick and choose their own vegetables can benefit from lower prices. The important lesson Harford makes is that it doesn't matter which supermarket you go to, but how you shop. Supermarkets are skilled at offering certain products at great value and other products with a significant price mark-up – and it is these expensive goods that are usually in the most convenient places for you to pick up.

Another tip for getting the best value is that sometimes these products are almost hidden away. **Robert H Frank**, in his 2007 book *The Economic Naturalist,* notes that the cheapest cappuccino at a popular coffee chain is the "short" cappuccino – which is not on

"If you want a bargain, don't try to find a cheap store. Try to shop cheaply. An expensive shopping trip is the result of carelessly choosing products with a high mark-up"
Tim Harford

Firms often try to budge us into "supersize" options that we don't really need.

the main menu. You have to be "in the know" to be able to order the short cappuccino. The point is, coffee shops and fast food restaurants try to nudge us into buying bigger – and more expensive – sizes. These bigger sizes are, of course, more profitable, because the marginal cost (the cost of one additional unit) of the ingredients is very low, but the higher prices are a way for a firm to target those consumers willing to pay. If we have our wits about us, we can reject the nudge toward bigger sizes and stick with the sizes we prefer.

Avoiding the default

Default options are a powerful influence on our decisions. **Richard Thaler** and **Cass Sunstein** originally investigated these with regard to health, but the principle of default option is also exploited by firms who wish to make us pay more. This is particularly relevant in markets such as electricity supply

or home insurance. Tim Harford argues that consumers have *choice aversion* because they fear that changing suppliers will have costs and a degree of uncertainty. This uncertainty causes us to stick with the default option – the supplier we currently have – even if changing might significantly reduce our annual bills. Firms exploit this customer inertia, often charging higher prices to existing long-term customers. By contrast, firms offer the cheapest tariffs to new customers – those who are willing to switch and are by definition the most price-sensitive. The lesson is that the default option can be a very expensive "choice". Some of the biggest savings can be made by looking at a price-comparison website and finding a new insurance deal/energy provider every year.

Can it be rational to be irrational?

Behavioural economists note that people exhibit many seemingly irrational behaviours, including *status quo bias* (preferring the current state of affairs), choice aversion and picking familiar items. However, **Vernon L Smith** (b. 1927), an American economist and Nobel Laureate, argues that it can be rational for consumers to seemingly violate laws of rational behaviour. In other words, all these consumer biases may be for a good reason. He notes that when shopping we have many *decision costs* – the costs of weighing up information, making a decision and then acting. Given all these aspects of shopping, it is not surprising we don't make a fully rational choice from the actual costs and benefits. If we worry about getting the best deal every time we go shopping, it can become a testing mathematical exercise. It may be far better to spend a little more on more expensive products but be able to finish quickly.

In other words, when we go shopping, getting the best price is only one factor out of many things to consider. Does it matter if your breakfast cereal is 10% cheaper at a supermarket five minutes farther away? Or that if you ignore the chance to switch insurance, it may cost you slightly more? In fact, instead of spending a couple of hours dealing with all the search costs and paperwork, you might be better off sitting outside in the garden and enjoying a stress-free life. Sometimes being too lazy to switch suppliers has an economic rationale.

Beware of special offers

An influential concept in behavioural economics is the idea of transaction utility (*see* page 73), developed by Richard Thaler. It explains why we can be easily swayed by sales.

If you ever go to buy a bed or mattress, you are likely to find that, very conveniently, the shop is having a sale on the very day you walk through the door! This 50% off sale achieves two things. In the first place, the initial high price acts as a signal to high quality. As **Dan Ariely** notes, we often correlate price with quality – we distrust very low prices and value goods that are expensive. Secondly, the sale makes us feel we are getting a bargain. We get acquisition utility (*see* page 73) from having a bed, but we also get transaction utility from feeling we beat the system and saved 50% over what we might have paid at another time. Because we shop for beds infrequently, we don't know the typical price of a bed or the fact that sales are near-permanent.

The problem is that the psychological effect of getting a sale item can encourage us to buy something that we don't really need. The classic is three-for-two deals, which can lead to unused food items as we have not rationally evaluated whether the items are good value.

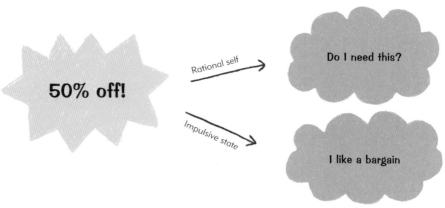

Faced with a bargain – two aspects of our nature can react in different ways.

Split personality

Daniel Kahneman argues that one issue with shopping is that we have a dual method for making decisions. Our first decision-making system is automatic, quick and intuitive; this part of us can be attracted by impulse buys and "sale" signs. The other decision-making system is cognitive, deliberate and controlled. A 2004 study by the economists Douglas Bernheim and Antonio Rangel put it in simpler terms. In a "hot state" we can make bad, emotional decisions that we later regret (such as to impulse-buy chocolate). In a "cold state", we make rational decisions and give ourselves time to weigh up the costs and benefits. The implication of this theory is not to go shopping when hungry. So before you jump in and spend $30,000 on your third sports car, walk away and come back in 20 minutes to check whether both elements of your nature really want to.

Another issue connected with shopping is that of mental accounting (*see* page 33). Richard Thaler developed this concept after realizing that money is not fungible – we don't treat all money the same. If we

Economic theory:

Behavioural economics suggests we have many cognitive biases – such as default options, choice aversion, mental accounting and an impulsive nature – that cause us to misspend.

had to pay our utility bill with cash, we would be more prone to switching to the cheapest supplier. But paying by card or by direct debit means that it is a question of out of sight, out of mind. Thaler argues that it is much easier to spend on a credit card because it is psychologically easier to make that transaction. Paying with cash has a greater impact on our decision-making. If we are prone to overspending, paying only in cash can be a way to moderate this, as it allows time for our impulsive side to be moderated by our more deliberate nature.

Making a decision:

We can learn a lot from behavioural economics if we find ourselves regretting purchases; the work of Thaler and Ariely may help us understand why we get caught up in bad decisions. However, Smith reminds us not to be too worried – sometimes we are better off making "imperfect" decisions if it helps us get the shopping over with as quickly as possible.

Work

Page 86: Should I go to college/university?

Page 91: Is it worth taking a promotion if it involves working long hours?

Page 95: How do I motivate my fellow workers?

Page 99: Do I benefit or suffer from immigration?

Page 104: Should I give up my secure job and work for myself?

Page 108: How can I get a pay rise?

Page 112: How can I be a good manager of people?

Page 116: Should I run my business just for profit?

Chapter 3

Should I go to college/university?

Gary Becker • Lester Thurow • Jacob Mincer • Michael Spence
Pierre Bourdieu • Richard B Freeman

In recent decades we have seen a steady expansion in college education across the world. But in this age of globalization and the proliferation of degrees, will you really be better off with a university degree if it means incurring the burden of a large student loan?

Benefits of a degree

The standard economic model for the benefits of education is framed through the *theory of human capital*, pioneered by **Gary Becker.** Becker's theory examines how education and training can improve a worker's human capital and thereby raise productivity. The important thing for students is that this model of human capital predicts that higher levels of education will bring better-paid jobs. Experience suggests this is true. According to the US Department of Education, in 2014 a Bachelor's degree gave a median annual salary of $49,900 – 66% higher than the median earnings of young high-school leavers ($30,000). Given this difference in wages, there is a clear financial case for taking a university degree.

Furthermore, education is not just about the prospect of greater productivity and a larger salary; higher education has the potential to give students non-monetary benefits from having more free time to gain a greater appreciation of culture and democracy. Economics professor Pedro Carneiro suggests that these benefits may be as diverse as "reduced crime, better parenting skills, and/or better health outcomes". A college degree is not just about being able to get on a prestigious management-training programme.

Calculating the cost

Yet before signing up for several years of student life and all this entails, it is worth considering the other side of the equation or, as economists call it, the *opportunity cost of education*. The concept of opportunity cost (*see* page 45) is intrinsic to an economic way of thinking. Gary Becker himself was aware of the high opportunity cost of education, when he stated that 75% of the private cost of education is income forgone as a result of spending three or four years in college.

A 2013 study by the Idaho Department of Labor suggested that the total financial cost of a four-year Bachelor's degree would be around $127,000 (while, incidentally, a two-year trade/vocational degree would cost $33,000). But, as Becker states, to this financial cost we need to add the opportunity cost of lost earnings.

Another factor worth bearing in mind is that if you're not academically minded but decide to keep studying, there is a risk that you'll drop out, which would leave you with the worst of both worlds – no degree *and* lost earnings. Just because your classmates would benefit from going to college doesn't mean you necessarily would.

Costs and benefits of going to college

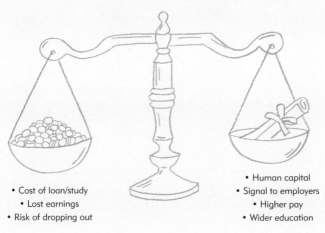

- Cost of loan/study
- Lost earnings
- Risk of dropping out

- Human capital
- Signal to employers
- Higher pay
- Wider education

On-the-job training

Furthermore, Becker notes that, in the real world, job skills are often not related to formal education levels. The problem with four years' studying is that it is four years in which you gain none of that on-the-job training. According to the American political economist **Lester Thurow** (1938–2016), the majority of workplace skills are acquired through on-the-job training, as opposed to formal education. Depending on the type of job, the quickest way to gain these relevant job skills is unlikely to be a degree in comparative psychology.

Yet before you jump into that first fast-food restaurant job at the age of 16, take note of a claim by the father of modern labour economics, the Polish–American economist **Jacob Mincer** (1922–2006). He contended that there is a clear link between education and lower levels of unemployment, arguing that an important reason for this is that workers with educational qualifications are more likely to receive on-the-job training. In other words, firms think it is less risky to invest in training for those workers with a past record of educational achievement. Experience seems to back this up. In 2016, the highest unemployment rate in the US was for those without any high school qualifications (7.4%). For those with a Bachelor's degree, the unemployment rate was just 2.7%.

"Human capital has become of much greater significance during the past two decades"
Gary Becker

"Economies need college graduates, but not college graduates only. They need a mix of skills."

Lester Thurow

The signals employers will read

The standard theory of human capital and education has been challenged by **Michael Spence.** He has argued that the primary role of higher education is not so much increasing labour productivity, but providing a signal that the person who takes the time to invest in education is a more able worker. In other words, your degree in economics plays little direct role in the skills of being a human resources manager, but your potential employer is impressed that if you have sat through three or four years of studying abstruse models of mainstream economics, you can probably survive corporate life and pick up what you need to learn. Of course, this model of signalling (*see* page 56) has implications for the social usefulness of higher education, but from the perspective of a student it doesn't really matter. In fact, it is a confirmation of why it is desirable to get more education – it is an important signal to potential employers.

This theory of signalling has been challenged by sociologists such as **Pierre Bourdieu**, who argued that human capital is more than simply education levels, as it includes less tangible factors such as social standing. Bourdieu noted that one reason better-educated people get paid higher wages is the fact that the middle classes are usually in a position to secure the best education. If this is true, it is not necessarily educational attainments that employers look at, but a wider range of factors, such as school, social class, race, gender, dress and even accent of speaking.

> ## Economic theory:
> The theory of human capital suggests that employees with more qualifications will gain higher-paid jobs. Therefore, in the long term, the benefits of education outweigh the initial costs.

In other words, if you have the right upbringing and social confidence, the signal of higher education may be less necessary.

Think outside the box

Kenneth Robinson, an international adviser on education, has argued that formal education kills creativity by encouraging a narrow focus of learning. In particular, Robinson would caution against a one-size-fits-all approach. Higher education may be beneficial for those who are academically oriented, but for artistic or entrepreneurial types it may be inappropriate. When discussing the merits of higher education, it is often pointed out that some of the great entrepreneurs and businessmen were high-school dropouts, including Thomas Edison, Richard Branson and Bill Gates.

We do know that Keynes never took a degree in economics. According to his biographer, Robert Skidelsky, "his total professional training came to little more than eight weeks. All the rest was learnt

> *"Education is the inculcation of the incomprehensible into the ignorant by the incompetent"*
> John Maynard Keynes

on the job". It is uncertain whether Keynes actually made the comment about education quoted above, but perhaps the lack of a formal economics degree helped Keynes think outside the box...

If you have the drive and imagination to start a business, there is another reason to be cautious about entering higher education. According to Larry Cordell, from the Federal Reserve Bank of Philadelphia, high student debt means that graduates struggle to invest in their small businesses, and therefore a college education with its accompanying student debt is "a drag on small business formation". If you have an entrepreneurial spirit, college education may impair rather than aid your chances.

Another issue to consider when deciding whether to study is what everyone else is doing. In the 1950s, university degrees were much rarer, and so getting a degree had greater *scarcity value* on wages, but in recent years the number of graduates has grown in the Western world. In the 1970s, **Richard B Freeman** (b. 1943) published *The Overeducated American*, which reflected how the *wage premium* for a graduate fell in the 1970s because of the increased supply in graduates. In other words, if everyone has a degree, the wage premium declines. However, Freeman's forecasts for graduates proved overly pessimistic – numerous researchers, to quote M Mendes de Oliveira et al., "found that employers tend to value and prize overeducation and at the same time penalize undereducation".

Student debt

Making a decision:
As Becker and Spence suggest, there is a strong financial incentive to go to college, in addition to all the non-financial benefits of study. However, if you are not particularly academic or you are impatient to set up a business, college is by no means necessary.

Is it worth taking a promotion if it involves working long hours?

Carl Menger • Bruno Frey • Max Weber • Thorstein Veblen • Richard B Freeman • Heather Boushey • Tibor Scitovsky • John Maynard Keynes • Benjamin Friedman • Karl Marx

Promotion typically brings higher pay, greater responsibility and more challenging (and possibly interesting) work. But is the extra income worth the increased pressure? Should we aspire to climb the greasy pole of promotion, or is satisfaction to be found in acceptance of our current job?

The first issue is the importance of salary. Mainstream economic theory equates higher income with higher utility. With a bigger salary, you will be able to consume more goods and services, such as a better holiday, a new car and more savings for retirement. From the perspective of maximizing consumption, the promotion will help.

However, economics also cautions against an automatic assumption that higher income equates to an equivalent increase in happiness. Diminishing marginal utility theory (*see* page 21), developed by **Carl Menger**, has been re-emphasized by many economists over the past century – precisely because it is such an important concept. Does an extra $10,000 a year from promotion actually make us happier? Well, perhaps for a few months, at least, but the extra income is likely to have rapidly diminishing utility.

When the pleasure wears off

Related to diminishing returns is the concept of *hedonic relativism*. Philip Brickman and Donald Campbell noted in 1971 that human happiness has a tendency to return to a relatively stable level, despite short-term events that may impact our happiness.

In other words, this rather fatalistic philosophy states that if our salary increases from $70,000 to $100,000, we may be a bit happier for a few months, but the gain in happiness soon falls back to the long-term average (the "dismal science" again). In other words, a promotion that gives a reward of extra money may be a temporary boost in satisfaction, but don't expect it to last.

Addicted to promotion

Another issue with being promoted is that once we get on the ladder, it may feed our desire for continual improvement. **Bruno Frey**, who has worked on happiness economics (*see* page 21), found that, although the marginal utility of extra income quickly dissipates, gaining one promotion soon creates the desire for further promotions. We get used to the "high" of getting promoted, but the joy is not in being in a better job, so much as in the process of getting promoted. No matter where we are in our career path, there's always someone better than we are – and it is this that leaves us dissatisfied. One promotion is never enough, so we have a continued desire to repeat the promotion.

Status and self-esteem

Sociologists take a different perspective on work, stressing the role of non-monetary factors in the rewards of work. The German political economist and sociologist **Max Weber** (1864–1920) introduced the concept of life chances. Weber argued that life chances are determined by social class, income and occupational status. Promotion is an opportunity to increase income but, more importantly, to improve occupational status and even social class. Weber realized that accepting a promotion is not just about the potential higher salary but the prestige of gaining a higher position in the workplace and society.

It is similar to the work by the economist and sociologist **Thorstein Veblen** (1857–1929). In his best-known book, *The Theory of the Leisure Class* (1899), he satirized the value that people placed on gaining higher social status and being able to display this to others in society. While noting the importance of social status (which a promotion may give), he was also very critical of an ostentatious display of status and wealth. (Veblen led by example – seemingly uninterested in promotions, he later moved to a Californian shack, to live in obscurity.)

However, we don't have to take Veblen's biting social satire to heart. Willingness to seek and accept promotion can affect our self-esteem in a positive way. The sociologist Robert K Merton argued that if a person has a broadly negative outlook on job prospects – feeling he is always doomed to work in low-pay, low-status employment – this can

> ## Economic theory:
> The substitution effect suggests work is more attractive if higher paid. However, the income effect suggests that with higher pay we would like to take more leisure.

become a self-reinforcing reality. By contrast, taking a promotion and behaving as if we expect to advance in our career can become a *self-fulfilling* prophecy. According to this philosophy of positive psychology, in seeking and accepting promotion we gain a sense of self-improvement, which helps to make continual improvements possible.

Sacrificing leisure and family time

A drawback of promotion is that higher income will require a trade-off involving more hours and responsibility, which presents a dilemma. Is it worth gaining a higher salary if it cuts into leisure and family time? The economist **Richard B Freeman** said, "The problem for the highly paid today is not that of finding a modest amount of work…but of finding ways to reduce pressures to work more."

John D Owen in *The Price of Leisure* (1969) noted that there is an *income effect* and a *substitution effect* of higher pay. The substitution effect states that higher wages encourage us to work more, while the income effect says that higher wages mean we can gain our target income through working less – and therefore enjoy more leisure. Owen notes that it can come down to personal preference. If we place a higher value on more leisure than on more pay, we will have to turn down a promotion.

On this theme, the American economist **Heather Boushey** (b. 1970) argues that modern families are struggling to deal with the rising number of work hours taken by both men and women. With women increasingly joining the labour force and seeking a career, it is harder to keep on top of household chores. Therefore, in the absence of affordable childcare facilities, a promotion that requires longer hours would have to be weighed against this opportunity cost (*see* page 45) of greater fatigue and less leisure time – especially for women, who are still more likely to be responsible for household tasks.

A free market economist might argue that having higher pay and fewer hours is not a problem if the higher wages enable a worker to outsource household tasks. In other words, promotion may enable you to pay for better childcare, a gardener and a cleaner. However, while the free market can, to some extent, deal with subtasks like cleaning and childcare, any parent will tell you there are some child-rearing tasks that just can't be sublet to market forces.

Tibor Scitovsky argues that the pursuit of higher income, and the inevitable rise in longer hours, has led to costs for society, such as dysfunctional families. The fact that social interaction and spending time with children cannot be outsourced to an agency makes people think twice about a promotion which takes more of a person's time.

If that doesn't give cause for concern, the researchers Chris Boyce and Andrew Oswald found a decline in the health of people who had been promoted. They discovered that getting a promotion "on average produces 10% more mental strain and gives up to 20% less time to visit the doctors".

Other factors

Not all economists view working more hours with distaste. Back in 1930, **John Maynard Keynes** predicted that his grandchildren's generation would be able to work just 15 hours a week. Keynes's logic was that rising productivity would enable people to choose shorter hours. Of course, this hasn't happened. In explaining why people work longer hours, the political economist **Benjamin Friedman** (b. 1944) argues that people may be happy to choose higher working hours because of the

substitution effect – with higher pay, work is more valuable. He also states that, "in an era of ever fewer settings that provide effective opportunities for personal connections and relationships", the workplace has become one of the most popular locations for personal connections and developing relationships.

In other words, work is about much more than an income–leisure trade-off. Work can have intrinsic value, giving varying degrees of utility. In an evaluation of jobs, pay is one factor out of many. Larger factors are the sense of job satisfaction and sense of identity within the work process. Scitovsky claims that responsibility gives more potential for real satisfaction because we are stretched into dealing with interpersonal conflicts and management, making a promotion desirable.

It also depends on how much you enjoy your current job. In the 19th century, **Karl Marx** noted the soul-destroying nature of capitalism, which gives boring repetitive jobs on highly specialized assembly lines. Ideally, Marx would have liked you to start a revolution of the proletariat, but if that seems slightly too daunting, you could just accept a promotion to a more interesting position, overseeing other workers.

A final, very practical issue when deciding whether to accept a promotion is whether you are able to do the job. The *Peter Principle* (formulated in 1969 by the educator and author Laurence J Peter) states that, in many organizations, people tend to get promoted until they reach their level of incompetence. It is based on the observation that promotion comes from past performance, but this may not be a guide to the future job. For example, if you are an excellent graphic designer or football player, it doesn't mean you necessarily will thrive as a manager of a design studio or football team.

Making a decision:

Promotion can give more responsibility and more satisfaction. Whatever economists may say about diminishing returns, extra money can always come in handy. If we are attracted by higher pay, we will take the promotion as Friedman might predict. However, taking on more hours and responsibility definitely has an opportunity cost of less non-work time. If we feel that promotion only increases our stress, we may take the work of Frey and Scitovsky to heart and prioritize our free time.

How do I motivate my fellow workers?

Michael C Jensen • Edward Lazear • Adam Smith • Richard B Freeman • George Akerlof
Carl Shapiro • Joseph Stiglitz • Tomasz Obloj • Dan Ariely • Abraham Maslow • Ernst Fehr

If you are a business owner managing a group of fellow workers, how do you inspire them to work hard when they don't display much enthusiasm? The orthodox response is typically to offer financial rewards for harder work. But to transform disgruntled workers into inspired co-workers may not always be as easy as offering cash incentives.

Many jobs have guaranteed pay and conditions, which means workers are not directly affected by their own productivity. In economics it is known as the *principal-agent problem*, a theory developed by the economists **Michael C Jensen** (b. 1939) and William Meckling. It states that the owner wants to maximize profits, but the workers don't – they just want to enjoy their time at work (which may involve shirking). The problem that managers face is how to motivate these workers, when they don't have a share in the outcome of a firm.

Financial incentives

The obvious solution, say economists, is performance-related pay. **Edward Lazear** (b. 1948), an economist credited with the creation of *personnel economics,* argues that there is empirical evidence to suggest incentives do increase productivity. Lazear found a glass-installation firm that, after it introduced piece rates (pay per job), saw a 44% rise in productivity. This is exactly what mainstream economic theory would predict – payment directly related to the job does increase worker productivity, as **Adam**

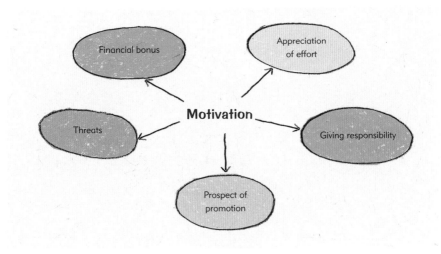

Smith stated in the 18th century. Lazear also found that incentives attract hard-working people to the job and encourage lazy people to leave (and save you the bother of managing them).

In some jobs, it is much harder to assess individual performance. But if individual performance-related pay is difficult, an alternative is to provide incentives based on the performance of the whole company. In the 2010 book *Shared Capitalism at Work,* edited by **Richard B Freeman**, Douglas Kruse and Joseph Blasi, there is strong evidence that share options and profit-sharing schemes help improve productivity. The principle is the same – giving workers a share in the company's fortunes changes their motivation.

George Akerlof viewed labour markets as a partial gift exchange. If you pay workers a minimal wage to get them to work, the worker will respond by giving minimum effort to avoid getting the sack. This led Akerlof to develop an *efficiency wage theory*, which states that paying a wage above the market equilibrium is an effective way to raise workers' morale and therefore productivity. **Carl Shapiro** (b. 1955) and **Joseph Stiglitz** (b. 1943), winner of a Nobel Memorial Prize, offered a variation on this theory, stating that it was the threat of being made unemployed that gave an incentive for workers to avoid shirking.

> **Economic theory:**
> Mainstream economic theory places emphasis on financial incentives to motivate workers, but recently economists have investigated non-financial incentives.

When financial incentives backfire

Tomasz Obloj (b. 1980) finds that financial incentives for employers can often become counterproductive and subject to diminishing returns as employees find ways to exploit the reward system. He gives a short example about the unintended consequences of incentives. In colonial India, the governor of Delhi paid a bounty on cobra skins to try to rid the city of the snakes. However, realizing it could be profitable, people responded by breeding cobras in captivity, killing them and then claiming the bounty. The number of snakeskins mushroomed, and the scheme was abandoned with more snakes than ever before.

In a more modern setting, **Dan Ariely** noted that when Wells Fargo bank set sales targets to employees, over time the workers

> *"Adding money to the equation can backfire and make people* less *driven"*
> Dan Ariely

realized they could meet their sales goals by opening fake accounts in their customers' names. As can be seen from this example, bonuses – rather than increasing motivation – can distort behaviour in a negative way.

Ariely states that money is just one factor out of many, and indeed workers can feel cash bonuses are essentially bribes and are ways to get them to do something they should be doing anyway. In some studies, Ariely noted, workers who received a cash bonus may have worked hard initially but the effect soon wore off. Investigating motivation effects at Intel, Ariely concluded that the attempts were counterproductive.

Other rewards

If not with pay, how can we motivate workers? James Malcomson argued that, if offering higher pay is not attractive (or a possibility), managers can use the chance of promotion to encourage motivation. If there is a periodic possibility of this, workers have an incentive to work hard and impress their boss. Malcomson likened it to a tournament – where workers try to win the prize of promotion. It doesn't have to be about higher pay – it could be about status and influence at work.

In his book *Hierarchy of Needs* (1943), the psychologist **Abraham Maslow** (1908–70) presented a broader understanding of the forces that

motivate workers. He argued that employers should look out for differing needs in their workers. Firstly, workers demand sufficient money to meet physical needs and to give them a sense of safety and security in work. After these basic requirements of life, workers are seeking a sense of belonging, esteem and a chance for *self-actualization* (fulfilling their potential); in other words, they crave the opportunity for creativity and problem-solving, and a chance to progress. The implication of this model is that after a basic salary, the way to motivate workers is to give them a sense of belonging, responsibility and a chance to influence their workplace.

Psychologists have posited that a crucial factor in determining worker satisfaction is the sense of achievement. The "Need for Achievement Theory", developed by David McClelland and J W Atkinson, argues that the real motivation for workers is the

Simplified hierarchy of needs

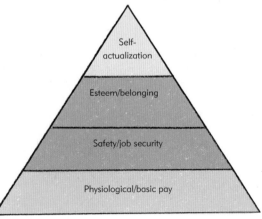

97

"Incentives are the essence of economics"
Edward Lazear

ability to gain a sense of achievement from work. This isn't a financial reward but job satisfaction from doing a good job. From a manager's point of view, the trick is to offer workers the chance to feel part of the process and reward hard work and good effort. Dan Ariely argues that it can be as simple as acknowledgement. It is simple, cheap but potentially very effective, and it is something all managers can do, even if they are powerless to set pay rates.

Fairness, trust and appreciation
In a workplace environment, it is often little things that matter. *Equity theory,* developed by the psychologist J Stacy Adams, suggests that a key factor in determining motivation is not so much the actual salary or type of work, but whether the worker feels fairly treated compared with others in the workforce. A skilled manager needs to be particularly aware of employers becoming disgruntled at a sense of unfair treatment, discrimination or lack of appreciation.

These ideas of a more holistic approach to worker motivation have become increasingly adopted by economists, especially in the realm of behavioural economics. Armin Falk and Michael Kosfeld found that placing higher levels of trust in the workforce is effective in increasing the workers' intrinsic motivation and performance. The interesting thing about this management approach is that it stands in stark contrast to bonuses or the threat of redundancy. By trusting employees we seek to make them feel part of the organization in a way that financial incentives may not achieve.

In "Fairness and Retaliation: The Economics of Reciprocity" (2000), the Austrian behavioural economist **Ernst Fehr** noted the importance of reciprocity between economic agents. If managers offer empathy and thoughtfulness to their employees, workers respond in kind. Similarly, small negative actions from a boss will elicit ill feeling in return.

The consequence of this for managers is to remember not to neglect the small, everyday issues – from listening to complaints about the temperature of the office, to offering generous praise.

Making a decision:
For some types of job, workers may respond well to financial incentives, as Lazear predicts. However, you may feel, like Ariely, that your co-workers would respond much better to appreciation and being given more responsibility for their work.

Do I benefit or suffer from immigration?

Paul Samuelson • Milton Friedman • Bryan Caplan • Alan Greenspan • D F Schloss
David Card • Gordon Hanson • Lant Pritchett • George Borjas

In an era of globalization, immigration is a hotly contested political issue. Putting the emotive aspects of immigration to one side, what is its economic impact? Does it put downward pressure on wages as critics suggest? Or does net migration actually benefit those already living in the country?

In his best-selling economics textbook, the American economist and Nobel Laureate **Paul Samuelson** (1915–2009) stated the simple economic logic that net migration leads to a higher supply of labour and therefore downward pressure on wages. Samuelson also noted that in the period 1950–65, when US immigration policy was quite restrictive, real wages rose rapidly. However, he explained that the impact of immigration was not equally distributed throughout the economy; it tended to benefit wealthy American business owners, who could profit from employing cheaper labour. By contrast, low-income native-born workers tended to see more job competition from the new arrivals, leading to fewer job positions and lower wages – all of which suggests we should share genuine concerns about large-scale migration.

The benefits question

Milton Friedman criticized immigration from a different perspective. From a libertarian (*see* page 12) point of view, Friedman supported open borders and argued that US immigration up to 1914 was generally a positive experience. However, he also stated that if a country had a welfare state, there was a clear financial incentive for people to move into that country, attracted by the prospect of receiving welfare benefits; Friedman even feared that, with open borders and a generous welfare state, the supply of immigrants would become infinite.

Paradoxically, he argued that the best solution was illegal immigration. Illegal immigrants could help the economy by increasing labour resources, but, being illegal, they wouldn't be entitled to welfare benefits, so the host nation would get the best of both

"There is no doubt that free and open immigration is the right policy in a libertarian state, but in a welfare state it is a different story: the supply of immigrants will become infinite"
Milton Friedman

worlds. Friedman seems to be suggesting that a country should have immigration laws, but not enforce them.

With youth on their side

However, other economists argue that it is a mistake to view immigrants as coming for benefits, when the vast majority are motivated by seeking better-paid jobs. The labour economists Christian Dustmann and Tommaso Frattini researched the effect of immigration and found that immigrants were net contributors to the government budget. For example, in 2001–11, immigrants from Eastern Europe made a net fiscal contribution of almost £5 billion to the UK economy. Immigrants help the fiscal position for various reasons. The most important factor is that they tend to be of working age and therefore pay income taxes but don't require pensions or as much health care. Also, contrary to media speculation, they are less likely to claim benefits or be eligible for social housing than native-born workers.

Bryan Caplan (b. 1971), an American welfare economist, makes a similar point, arguing that US welfare spending is focused on the old and not on the working poor. Since immigrants tend to be young, they make tax contributions, which support the native-born elderly rather than "milking the system" as Friedman feared. This argument is particularly relevant given the aging populations seen across the Western world. Japan, with some of the most restrictive immigration laws, has seen a falling birth rate,

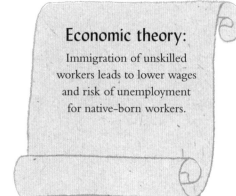

Economic theory:

Immigration of unskilled workers leads to lower wages and risk of unemployment for native-born workers.

a rapidly aging population and the highest national debt as a percentage of GDP in developed economies. Immigration is often presented as a solution for dealing with a rapidly aging society.

The American economist **Alan Greenspan** (b. 1926), who was chairman of the US Federal Reserve from 1987 to 2006, argued that immigration (often illegal) made a significant contribution to American economic growth in 2000–7, with benefits outweighing costs.

Increasing the demand for labour

Another important issue is that it is a mistake to concentrate on the effect of immigration on labour supply. Back in 1891 the British economist **D F Schloss** (1850–1912) developed the so-called *lump of labour fallacy* – the contention that the amount of work in an economy is fixed. People making this assumption fear that immigrants will "take jobs from native workers", but Schloss argued that this is not what happens. Migrants may

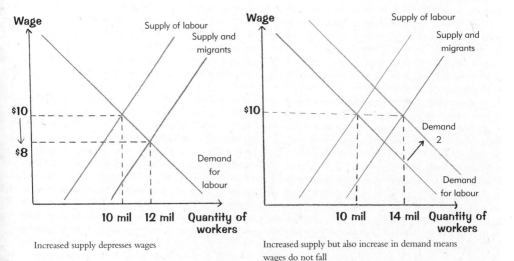

Increased supply depresses wages

Increased supply but also increase in demand means wages do not fall

take jobs, but they will also increase demand for goods and services, create new businesses and encourage firms to invest in more capital.

In other words, Paul Samuelson was mistaken to consider only the impact on labour supply; he should also have looked at the effect of migration on the increasing demand for labour. This explains why the large-scale immigration into the US in the past 150 years has also corresponded to a significant increase in real wages and living standards. There is definitely no link between immigration and long-term unemployment rates.

The Canadian labour economist **David Card** (b. 1956) investigated the effect of 100,000 migrants coming to Florida from Cuba during the 1981 boatlifts. He found that, despite the very rapid and unexpected migration, it did not cause unemployment or depress wages. It seemed that Florida had the capacity to absorb this rapid flow of immigration with little adverse impact. Card admits he was surprised at his own findings.

Rachel Friedberg examined another natural experiment – the very high levels of migration to Israel of 600,000 Russian Jews in the early 1990s. She found that Russian migrants tended to compete for the lowest-paid jobs and, if anything, had a positive impact on the wages of native-born Israelis. Friedberg suggests that immigrants are not perfect substitutes for native workers (owing to language differences) and that immigration has a positive effect on labour demand as well as increasing labour supply.

Boosting innovation

Another benefit of immigration, according to the American economist **Gordon Hanson** (b. 1964), is that immigrants are likely to improve rates of innovation and help boost creativity in the economy. Hanson argues that immigrants have a wider range of social and cultural capital and are more likely to study sciences and engineering and to develop patents.

Douglas McWilliams, a British economist, argues that cosmopolitan cities such as London and New York that can attract migrant labour become hubs of creativity, and are a key factor in the success of the new IT-based "flat-white economy" with its start-ups and entrepreneurial small businesses.

Who benefits and who loses?

According to the American development economist **Lant Pritchett** (b. 1959), completely open borders around the world would increase GDP by a staggering $65 trillion. This reflects a general consensus among economists that immigration can increase the GDP of economies. However, the impact of immigration is still contentious because, although migration may increase overall GDP, there is no guarantee that all sections of society benefit in the same way.

George Borjas (b. 1950), an American labour economist, is sceptical about the benefits of immigration. In particular, unskilled native-born workers such as high school dropouts are negatively affected by the immigration of low-skilled workers, who increase competition for low-paid jobs. To Borjas, immigration (along with other factors such as trade and the decline of unions) explains the relatively poor labour-market prospects of the low-skilled in recent decades.

In fact, we need to consider more than just wages and jobs. Living standards are determined by the availability of housing and access to local amenities. Immigration tends to be highly concentrated in particular areas, and this can cause congested social services and push up housing prices – especially in cities with limited space for increasing supply. Albert Saiz, who specializes in urban and housing economics, found that an increase in immigration of 1% is equivalent to a 1% increase in house rents or prices. This is another example of the unequal effects of immigration. The wealthy benefit from the lower prices of taxi services and childcare, while those on low incomes experience potentially higher living costs and lower wages.

Making a decision:

Borjas and Samuelson suggest that large-scale migration of low-skilled workers will harm the wages and prospects of similarly low-paid workers. Therefore, if you are low-skilled, you are more likely to experience immigration as a cost. However, David Card offers a more optimistic view of immigration and points to the way the labour market can absorb migrants without depressing wages, and, as Gordon Hanson argues, in the long term, immigration may boost innovation and cultural diversity.

"*Limitation of the supply of any grade of labour relative to all other productive factors can be expected to raise its wage rate*"

Paul Samuelson

Should I give up my secure job and work for myself?

Milton Friedman • Karl Marx • Steven Levitt • David Blanchflower • Andrew Oswald
Dan Ariely • Ross Levine • Gerald Friedman • Edward Lazear

There is a famous Monty Python sketch where a chartered accountant of 20 years comes to a career adviser, bored out of his mind from working as an accountant, and announces he would like to try his hand at being a lion tamer. Despite its comic absurdity, it echoes a deep longing many employees have to jack in their job and try something completely different. What would economists advise about giving up a secure job and seeking self-employment?

A free market economist like **Milton Friedman** believes that every employee is a potential capitalist waiting to exploit their own potential. If you feel that you have the skills to set up your own business, you should maximize your human capital (*see* page 86) and enter the free market. Friedman was an advocate of small-business entrepreneurship because when people are free to work for themselves, they have a much stronger incentive to work hard, be productive and innovate. If working for a large firm feels demoralizing and lacking in incentives, then you will never maximize your potential. If you are dismayed by how your firm is managed and think you can do better, why not try?

Reading the writings of **Karl Marx** may, ironically, bring you to a similar conclusion. The Marxist analysis of work in a capitalist economy is one of exploitation and alienation. True, Marx hopes that the exploited workers of the world will start a revolution rather than seek self-employment.

The trade-off

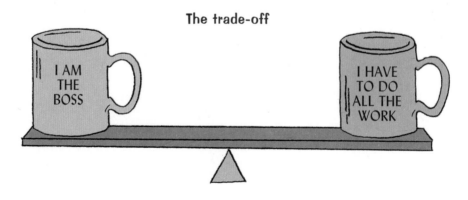

I AM THE BOSS

I HAVE TO DO ALL THE WORK

But, if you can't beat 'em, join 'em. If you feel you are treated like a commodity at work, don't just complain – try something different. In the words of Marx, "you have nothing to lose but your chains".

Does self-employment make you better off?

However, before you resign from the office, take note of the findings of the economist Barton H Hamilton, who in 2000 researched the rewards of self-employment and found that the self-employed typically have lower earnings. Furthermore, their average earnings are distorted by a handful of "superstar" entrepreneurs. If we ignore the small percentage of self-employed who become very successful, the median earnings are lower than similar positions in employed work. The problem is that these "superstar" entrepreneurs – such as Bill Gates and Steve Jobs – are the ones who stick in our collective memory. We don't see the media profile of the thousands of self-employed struggling to keep their heads above water.

Drug-dealing is one extreme form of self-employment. In *Freakonomics* (2005), the economist **Steven Levitt** and the writer Stephen J Dubner investigated why many drug-dealers live with their mothers. The reason is that the pay structure is hierarchical. The "foot soldiers" of drug dealing are paid very low wages but are attracted to the job by the possibility of getting promoted and becoming a highly paid "manager". Crack dealing is obviously an illegal form of self-employment, which is, of course, not recommended, but it illustrates how the attraction of self-employment is not so much the average salary, as the possibility of being a "superstar" entrepreneur.

Hamilton reports that the self-employed gain a median income that is 35% less than a corresponding wage in the employed sector. Furthermore, the self-employed have additional costs, such as lack of income when on vacation or when ill, funding health care and advertising for work. Despite lower wages, the self-employed also tend to work longer hours. So what is the attraction of self-employment if we get lower wages, greater job insecurity and longer hours?

The British economists **David Blanchflower** (b. 1952) and **Andrew Oswald** (b. 1953) found that business owners report greater job satisfaction than employed workers. It is the freedom to be one's own boss that is one of the most attractive aspects of self-employment. Even if we work 50 or 60 hours a week, at least we are working for ourselves. It is easier to work long hours when it is our own decision and we are in a position to decide the direction of the

"Entrepreneurship offers the possibility of comparably enormous increases in earnings"
Ross Levine and Yona Rubinstein

business. The sense of ownership and control is significant in determining our motivation and job satisfaction.

Dan Ariely argues that monetary compensation is only one of many aspects that motivate us to work. The real motivation comes from a sense of self-actualization (*see* page 97) and purpose. Whatever happens to our own business, we are motivated in a way that does not occur in employment. If you feel underappreciated and undervalued, at least with self-employment you have the chance to mould the job into something that reflects your own values. These important non-pecuniary benefits of self-employment make it attractive despite lower pay.

However, the American economist **Ross Levine** (b. 1960) is more optimistic about the prospects of entrepreneurs to earn higher wages than in employment. He makes the point that self-employment includes a diverse range of jobs, from starting up a business to selling hot dogs, which is little different to employment. Separating these different types of self-employment, Levine shows that the self-employed who set up their own companies earn about 18% more than they were earning as salaried employees.

The gig economy

In recent years, this division within the ranks of the self-employed has become more marked with the rise of the *gig economy* (which utilizes a high proportion of freelance or short-term-contract labour in a diffused labour force). It reflects the fact that workers often take on self-employed work as part

> ## Economic theory:
> Self-employment gives greater incentives for individuals than employment. It can also enable them to use all their talents in creating more meaningful work.

of a portfolio of jobs. For example, they might work for a taxi company, but also work in a self-employed capacity for Uber or a delivery company. To supporters of flexible labour markets such as the journalist Thomas Friedman, this gives workers greater flexibility, the opportunity to choose the hours they work and fulfilment through a balanced portfolio of interesting jobs.

However, critics of labour market deregulation such as **Gerald Friedman** (b. 1955) argue that the gig economy is really a way for firms to avoid labour costs such as healthcare insurance, and even to pay less than the national minimum wage. He also notes that those self-employed workers in the gig economy have very few rights or the ability to complain or bargain with firms. While some may like the flexibility over employment, many others find the uncertainty over pay and conditions a major source of stress, which leads to a decline in the quality of life. According to Gerald Friedman, self-employment in this new gig

economy is the worst of both worlds – with lower pay but without the compensating benefits of being in control of the business.

Although self-employed contracts may offer a poor return, for most entrepreneurs it is not the kind of self-employment they aspire to anyway, as it is merely a disguised form of employment with lower benefits. If we wish to start our own business, what factors may determine our relative success? Ross Levine examined successful entrepreneurs and found they usually shared several attributes; these included scoring highly on learning aptitude tests, but also a willingness to "break the rules" and engage in illicit activities as teenagers. In other words, it suggests that a successful entrepreneur is one who is willing to take risks and has the confidence to try a road less travelled. The rewards and costs of self-employment are more extreme and may suit a risk-taker more than a risk-averse worker.

Who succeeds?

The American economist **Edward Lazear**, a founder of the field known as personnel economics, examined business creators and found that the most successful entrepreneurs were those with a wide range of skills and experience. They were not necessarily outstanding in any one field but were competent in all aspects required to be a business owner. The archetypal scientific genius may come up with a great invention, but if his genius is not matched with basic admin skills, he may make a poor entrepreneur – which perhaps explains why some scientific geniuses die penniless. If you want to be a successful business owner, it may be more important to be a jack-of-all-trades than a real genius or specialist.

Making a decision:

If you are dissatisfied with your current job and you feel you could do better yourself, Milton Friedman would encourage you to follow your instincts. But as Lazear cautions, make sure you know what you are letting yourself in for. If you do go for self-employment, Gerald Friedman would advise making sure you don't end up in a gig economy, working for less with no compensating benefit.

How can I get a pay rise?

Knut Wicksell • Peter F Drucker • George Akerlof • Janet Yellen
Gary Becker • Milton Friedman • Joseph Stiglitz • Joan Robinson
Adam Smith • Noam Chomsky • John Forbes Nash, Jr

We all feel we deserve a pay rise but what is the best way to go about getting one? Economics tells us a lot about how wages are determined but not necessarily how we can convince our boss to pay us a higher wage. However, a knowledge of the relevant economic principles may give us the confidence to claim the salary we deserve.

Knut Wicksell (1851–1926) – known as the "economist's economist" for synthesizing the early work of classical economists (based on free markets, free trade and rational consumers seeking value for money) such as Léon Walras and David Ricardo – developed a *theory of wage determination*. This stated that a worker should be paid according to their *marginal revenue product (MRP)*, which is the amount they produce multiplied by the price of the good. If they work hard and can produce more widgets per hour, they have a good claim for getting higher pay. There is a strong link between productivity and pay because rising output means employers can afford to pay higher wages.

Looking beyond productivity

However, the theory of MRP is not so applicable to the modern economy, where a worker's output is less tangible. **Peter F Drucker** (1909–2005), a management theorist, argued that in our modern *knowledge economy* (focused on service-sector industries such as education, IT, design) our job task is less easily definable. In this case, the practical solution is to develop a wider range of skills, such as being good with people and meeting all those management clichés like being a "goal-oriented team player".

If you have a boss who may be swayed by economic theory, you could even try mentioning the efficiency wage theory (*see* page 96) of **George Akerlof** and **Janet Yellen** (b. 1946), which they developed in 1986. They argue that higher wages increase productivity and loyalty to a firm so much that, in many circumstances, it can be profitable to increase wages because the productivity gains of happy workers outstrip any costs. The problem with presenting this efficiency wage theory is you are basically implying that you're not trying hard enough at the moment because you think your pay is too low.

However, some economists suggest that the most important factor behind getting a higher wage is simply the willingness to act. For example, one reason suggested for the gender wage gap is that women are less likely to initiate negotiations for higher pay, as identified in a 2005 study by Hannah Riley Bowles, Linda Babcock and Lei La. However, their study showed mixed results and suggested that, for women, simply being willing to ask for pay rises may not be enough, because bosses may respond differently to women asking for a pay rise.

Changing jobs

Even if we impress the boss with our engaging character and workplace demeanour, plus our wide skill set, and we ask very nicely for a pay rise, they may still be able to refuse by claiming it's not up to them anyway. If we are met with flat refusals, what options do we have?

In that situation, free market economists such as **Gary Becker** or **Milton Friedman** would suggest turning to the power of the market. If your job is genuinely underpaid, the only solution is to seek a higher wage in another job. If your employer really values you, even the threat of leaving may be sufficient to make them offer you a raise, but if your boss refuses, find an employer who will pay you more.

This *theory of competitive labour markets* is all very well, but finding a better-paid job is much more difficult in practice. **Joseph Stiglitz** recognized that there can be substantial problems in finding a new job, owing to the high search costs, interviews and uncertainty involved. In other words, free market theory may be of limited comfort to those struggling to get a higher wage.

Because of all the difficulties of finding a new job, many firms have a degree of monopsony power over us. This concept of *monopsony* was developed in 1933 by **Joan Robinson** (1903–83), an unorthodox British economist. She noted that many employers had the market power to set wages – and, unsurprisingly, set them lower than our MRP. It wasn't just Karl Marx who railed at the exploitation of labour as a commodity – even **Adam Smith** noted back in the 18th century that in setting wages the employer has the upper hand.

"Conventional wisdom (e.g., 'it pays to ask' and 'the squeaky wheel gets the grease') suggests that, if women want the same resources and opportunities as men, then they should learn to seek out, rather than shy away from, opportunities to negotiate"
H R Bowles, L Babcock and L Lai

Noam Chomsky (b. 1928) takes a similarly pessimistic view and has argued that modern capitalism creates a form of wage slavery where the odds are stacked against workers, especially those who are low-skilled. However, there is hope, because if firms have monopsony power, they are currently making profits at our expense – which means they can afford to pay higher wages. We just need a way to persuade them to do so.

Will joining a union help?

If firms have monopsony power, workers can try to provide a counterbalance – by organizing to form a trade union. Within a union, workers have greater bargaining power and the potential to demand higher wages.

In the post-war period, Milton Friedman found that trade unions were very successful at getting higher wages for union members than for non-union members. In fact, in the 1980s, free market economists like Friedman inspired Margaret Thatcher and Ronald Reagan to pursue a *supply side* revolution (free market reforms) which involved limiting the power of trade unions.

Friedman's research suggests that if you want to get a higher wage, you should persuade all the workers in your firm to join a trade union and then threaten your

> **Economic theory:**
> Marginal revenue product theory suggests there is a strong link between pay and productivity, so increasing productivity is key to a pay rise.

boss that, without a pay rise, you will all go on strike. (Whether Friedman thinks trade unions increase economic efficiency is another issue.)

But what makes a successful strike? Can collective bargaining really increase pay? If workers appear determined and well-organized, the employer may give in and pay a higher wage. However, if the employer feels he can split the workforce and survive a strike, he may reject their demands. It becomes a type of game theory – where the outcome depends on how the other agent responds.

The great US mathematician **John Forbes Nash, Jr** (1928–2015), developed a theory that the outcome will be in equilibrium at the point where neither party will be able

> *"Masters are always and everywhere in a sort of tacit, but constant and uniform, combination, not to raise the wages of labour above their actual rate"*
> Adam Smith

The economist Lawrence J Haber, who investigated game theory in wage negotiations for the Major League Baseball Players Association, had a word of caution as regards pursuing excessively confrontational tactics. He found that a key factor in successful wage negotiations was developing a sense of trust through exercising restraint.

Increasing your own value

At any rate, the hope of organizing unions in a modern gig economy (*see* page 106) may be limited. In this case, a neoclassical economist such as Gary Becker would stress the importance not of unionization but of individual human capital (*see* page 86). In other words, if you want higher pay, concentrate on increasing your skills, qualifications and adaptability. Taking on vocational training also acts as a signal that you are willing and able to learn. This is perhaps the most practical path to promotion and higher pay. And it's a lot easier than trying to form a union.

to gain by changing their strategy, given what the other party is doing. The problem is that gaining a *Nash equilibrium* may be suboptimal for both parties. In other words, to get a pay rise of, say, 2%, you have to spend a week on strike where you receive no pay and a good deal of ill will into the bargain. Workers know that if they don't go on strike, they won't get a pay rise. But equally the firm can't afford to give in easily because it is thinking not just about this pay rise but about discouraging strike action in the future.

Making a decision:

We may agree with Gary Becker that our best hope is to increase our productivity, such as by gaining more qualifications. However, if we feel that our boss is a monopsony, as Robinson describes, we may need to take a different approach, such as bargaining from within a trade union.

How can I be a good manager of people?

Adam Smith • David Ricardo • Dan Ariely • Paul Milgrom •Theodore Levitt
Vilfredo Pareto • Warren G Bennis • Daniel Kahneman

Even if you don't manage a company, you are most likely in a position of managing people, even if it is within your own family. What are the secrets of a successful manager? How can you get the best out of people? And can economic theory offer any insights into the management of staff?

Division of labour

In *The Wealth of Nations*, **Adam Smith** observed how a pin factory split up the production process into different jobs. This principle is known as the *division of labour*, and it enables managers to assign workers to specialize in the jobs at which they are relatively best. This principle is important for any organization. Suppose you are a parent of a family of five, and you know that you're the most able at doing a whole range of jobs, from making the meals to doing the financial accounts to cleaning the house. Does that mean you should do everything? No, you should still find a way to delegate some tasks to your partner and children.

This process of assigning jobs to the right person has a close parallel to the *theory of comparative advantage*. **David Ricardo** argued that countries should specialize in producing goods at which they are relatively best. The importance of this is that, even if a country has an absolute advantage in producing everything, it doesn't mean that it should actually try to produce everything itself. You specialize in what you are relatively best at. Therefore, in a family you may find yourself specializing in doing the tax return, but on

that particular day you should definitely delegate cleaning to your partner – even if you know that they aren't as good as you at it!

Effective delegation

If you are managing workers in a company, effective delegation becomes an essential component of your job. If your primary job is to come up with a business plan and to manage workers, don't spend your time ordering the stationery. Delegation is about more than just specializing in our relative strengths – it is also about giving responsibility and a sense of importance to other workers.

In evaluating worker motivation, **Dan Ariely** states that a key factor is whether workers can gain a sense of job satisfaction from being able to do a job with a degree of empowerment and responsibility. In other words, if you have the confidence to delegate responsibility and trust, then workers are likely to respond with greater loyalty to you and to the firm. A boss who is condescending and who tries to micromanage everything not only will suffer from burnout but also will irritate workers under him. Being a good manager means we need to focus on our most important tasks and responsibilities and trust those around us.

Ariely's findings are similar to those of **Paul Milgrom**, who evaluates business management. He argues that to get the best out of workers it is necessary to place fewer restrictions on them. In particular, he notes that modern manufacturing methods have a focus on smaller inventories, speedier service and greater flexibility. But for these more cost-effective strategies to work, management must not become too hierarchical. If every decision has to go through a manager, the system becomes inflexible and prone to bottlenecks.

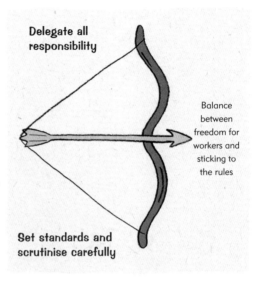

Delegate all responsibility

Balance between freedom for workers and sticking to the rules

Set standards and scrutinise carefully

Team spirit

Another area of concern for Milgrom is how to deal with the dichotomy between performance and incentives. He notes that in modern workplaces, most workers have a variety of goals. If performance is rewarded for a narrow achievement, then it will distort working practices to focus only on that. For example, there is an idea that teachers should receive performance-related pay based on test results or student evaluation. Milgrom, however, felt this would lead to unintended consequences – teachers would focus on maximizing test scores and ignore the wider dimensions of student achievements, such as creativity and thinking outside the box. A good manager needs to enhance the underlying attitude to the company, and encourage a team spirit rather than a competitive approach based on a narrow set of goals.

Leadership skills

Theodore Levitt (1925–2006), an American economist, cautioned against a managerial style that is too open. He said that creating ideas is the easy part – the real skill of a manager is the ability to deliver practical customer satisfaction. To Levitt, excess creativity "may be more of a millstone than a milestone". He said that ideas are easy to come by, but if you get too many ideas, the business loses focus; the real scarcity is of

"In the knowledge economy, the workplace relies heavily on trust, engagement, and goodwill"
Dan Ariely

people with the energy and staying power to implement ideas effectively.

On a similar theme, management experts often refer to the *80/20 rule*. This is a concept developed by the Italian economist **Vilfredo Pareto**, who noted that 20% of the population owned 80% of the wealth. The principle can also be applied in management, by using the rule of thumb that possibly 80% of the productivity of your business comes from perhaps 20% of your workforce and working practices. This can provide a way to recognize and challenge the less productive elements and concentrate more on those producing 80% of your success.

Also, while some stress the importance of delegating responsibility and "worker empowerment", Levitt emphasized the importance of strong leadership. The boss has to set the example for the rest of the company. Either consciously or unconsciously, people follow the lead of the person in charge. In popular parlance, we talk about "leading by example" and we say, "don't ask others to do what you wouldn't do yourself". Delegation is all very well, but without some leadership others will flounder.

Warren G Bennis (1925–2014), an American leadership consultant, coined the term *adhocracy*. It means that managers

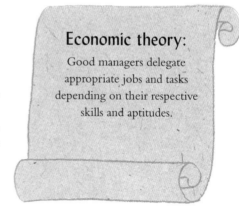

Economic theory:
Good managers delegate appropriate jobs and tasks depending on their respective skills and aptitudes.

need to be prepared to lead, while also using the principles of delegation, flexibility and willingness to change.

Behavioural factors

Daniel Kahneman has investigated the psychological factors that can influence effective management techniques. One consideration is that good managers and good leaders are likely to have an optimistic approach to work, business and other people.

Kahneman observes that if managers are subject to an irrational, or even delusional, optimism bias (*see* page 53), this may turn out to be a good thing. If we overrate our

"Confidence in their future success sustains a positive mood that helps them obtain more resources from others, raise the moral of their employees and enhance their prospects of prevailing"
Daniel Kahneman

Management styles

Work harder

You're doing such a good job

I'll let you get on with the job – you're the expert

capacities, it encourages us to take risks. By contrast, if a more pessimistic and cautious manager spreads pessimism throughout the business, it will damage prospects. In traditional economic theory, emotions and psychological outlook rarely get much of a mention, but if you have ever worked for a boss who is pessimistic and highly critical, you will know it is not particularly inspiring. Creating the right kind of atmosphere is critical for encouraging a good attitude to work.

Dan Ariely argues that we are heavily influenced by our environment, and a few small tweaks can nudge people into more productive work. He reports that what the most productive computer programmers have in common is that they work in an environment free from distraction. We all know that talkative colleagues, internet browsing, even a cluttered workplace can severely limit our productivity and focus. Ariely notes that good management may be about having the confidence to remove distractions – even if people have become used to them. He argues that the four biggest distractions are meetings, email, multitasking and structured procrastination – where people find small, fiddly jobs to do, rather than the crucial task at hand.

Making a decision:

Ariely suggests that the key is to give workers a sense of job satisfaction, which may involve appreciation and room for creativity. Levitt, on the other hand, stresses strong leadership, which according to Kahneman should include a sense of optimism and positivity.

Should I run my business just for profit?

Milton Friedman • Adam Smith • E F Schumacher • Joseph Stiglitz • Gary Becker

What is the purpose of work and business? Should we endeavour to maximize profits for our company and its shareholders or should we have a sense of social responsibility and try to maximize other objectives apart from profit? To some extent, we can do both at the same time – social responsibility can be a good business strategy. But if we are faced with the dilemma of whether to sacrifice profits in order to promote social responsibility, what do economists advise?

Milton Friedman argues that if you run a business, your only social responsibility is to maximize profits for your employers – the shareholders. He argues that any attempt to consider wider social implications, ranging from charitable concerns to workers or the environment, is misplaced. He argues that, whether you are a manager or a worker, you have no right to foist your preferences or your personal notions of social responsibility onto the business. If you have social responsibilities, you can do this in an individual capacity but not through the intermediary of a business.

Friedman argues that those who run or manage a business with regard to social responsibility are just using someone else's money to pursue their own concept of what is good. He claims that it is like deciding to place a tax on your own company and then choosing how to spend the tax money. According to Friedman, this is the government's role and it is wrong to try to determine the public good yourself.

Friedman comes very much from the classical school of economics (*see* page

10) and the tradition of **Adam Smith** which argues that if firms pursue their own profit-maximizing interests it will have the impact of maximizing social welfare. To Friedman, if you maximize a firm's profits, it will lead to more tax revenue, which the government can spend on public goods. When the government spends money, the areas of spending are decided, in theory, by the democratic process. But, if you take decisions to make less profit and divert resources yourself, then, in Friedman's words, you become a self-selected, undemocratic "legislator, executive and jurist". It is strong stuff from Friedman and it comes back to a firm belief in the effectiveness of free markets to create the most efficient outcome. Overall, Friedman is sceptical of our ability to outperform the free market and the simple goal of profit maximization.

There's more to life than profit

Friedman's faith in profit maximization stands in stark contrast to the philosophy of other economists, who argue that it is a mistake for business executives and managers solely to maximize profit. One prominent thinker who challenged this view of free markets and profit maximization was the German-born British economist **E F Schumacher**. He argued that those working in business have a responsibility to consider the public interest and not profit. To Schumacher, businesses who maximize profits are effectively working in the interests of a few wealthy small shareholders, leading to an inequitable distribution of resources.

Schumacher also contended that if we work for a firm, we will know best how the decisions of our business affect the stakeholders, such as workers, local communities and consumers. We will understand how to effectively promote social welfare instead of relying on national government regulation and taxation. If we see effective ways to improve social welfare, we should do it, not hope it is done by an *invisible hand*. As **Joseph Stiglitz** once quipped, "Adam Smith's invisible hand – the idea that free markets lead to efficiency as if guided by unseen forces – is invisible, at least in part, because it is not there."

Different objectives for firms

Profit is the only goal for business

If we are "nice" more people will buy our products

Saving the planet is more important than making money for shareholders

"There is one and only one social responsibility of business – to use its resources and engage in activities designed to increase its profits so long as it stays within the rules of the game"
Milton Friedman

Costs of profit maximization

In the credit bubble of 2000–6, profit maximization strategies encouraged executives, managers and workers to sell as many mortgages as possible. Salesman were paid on commission, so there were efforts to legally sell unsustainable mortgages without regard for the consequences. This led to personal hardship for those who later couldn't afford the repayments on their mortgages and it also contributed to the economic crash. Stiglitz argues that short-termism and profit orientation can lead to damage to society in the long run. Ultimately many mortgage companies went bankrupt after the credit bubble. Therefore, there is a clear personal and social responsibility to consider the wider implications and ignore the temptation of profit maximization. In the case of mortgage selling, we can't rely on government regulation, as the industry is evolving faster than governments can keep up.

Friedman contends that profit will be taxed by governments and spent on public goods. In reality, however, corporations have been successful in increasingly avoiding corporation tax through offshore accounts and funnelling money through countries with low tax rates. Stiglitz has criticized multinational companies for finding ways to avoid paying corporation tax, which leads, needless to say, to lower tax revenue. Therefore, a strict policy of seeking to maximize profit for shareholders can lead to a decline in social welfare.

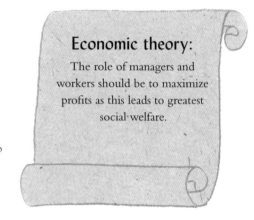

Economic theory:
The role of managers and workers should be to maximize profits as this leads to greatest social welfare.

Corporate responsibility

The economist Markus Kitzmuller, who has investigated the role of *corporate social responsibility*, asks us to consider two types. The first involves firms adopting "socially responsible" behaviour in a way that helps promote the long-term profitability of a firm. This is an approach pioneered by **Gary Becker** – examining our decisions from the perspective of economic costs and benefits. For example, if a firm gives money to charity, supports public goods and incurs higher costs to look after the environment and workers, this can be popular with consumers and workers and cements the "brand image" of a firm. It is sometimes known as the *halo effect*. Companies that create positive images can help boost long-term demand. By contrast, firms perceived as unthinking profit maximizers, as in the model advocated by Milton Friedman, could be subject to customer boycotts or damaging public relations. Also, the economist David P Baron argues that there are cases where

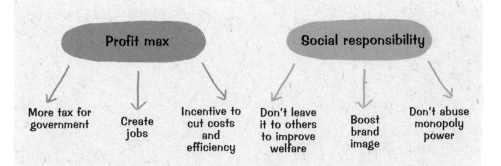

Profit max			Social responsibility		
More tax for government	Create jobs	Incentive to cut costs and efficiency	Don't leave it to others to improve welfare	Boost brand image	Don't abuse monopoly power

firms may exhibit voluntary restraint to discourage future legislation. For example, by voluntarily doing better than the minimum legal requirement, the firm may avoid future regulations and costs.

The second type of corporate social responsibility Kitzmuller identifies is when the costs are much greater than the benefits of the halo effect. Should we pursue social responsibility even at the cost of lower profits and possible higher prices? The American economist Forest L Reinhardt observes that if managers engage in unsustainable social responsibility, they could put the firm in danger from the falling market share and falling profits and could even put their jobs on the line. For example, if we run a business and keep on unproductive workers because we don't want to make people unemployed due to the social costs, we could put the viability of the business at risk. In this case, it presents a difficult dilemma. Kitzmuller argues that if we sacrifice profit, and if shareholders don't share our social concerns, then it is a form of moral hazard (see page 68) – we are acting differently from the interests of the owners.

However, Schumacher argues that it is only when we can act in a way that is considerate and altruistic that we will gain true satisfaction from work and business. If we are tied to a limited perspective of profit maximization, then we will feel more alienated.

Making a decision:
Milton Friedman makes a strong case to ignore social responsibility and concentrate on maximizing profits for your firm. However, you may feel like Kitzmuller that corporate social responsibility can be an effective way for a firm to prosper in the long term. If this still makes you feel uneasy, you could follow Schumacher's advice that your job is not profit maximization for a small number of shareholders but to act in the widest interests of society.

Finance

Page 122: How do I beat the market?

Page 126: How do I survive inflation?

Page 132: How can I make my small business more profitable?

Page 136: How much should I put into retirement savings?

Page 140: How do I avoid getting caught by financial bubbles?

Page 144: How much personal debt should I take on?

Chapter 4

How do I beat the market?

Daniel Kahneman • Amos Tversky • Eugene Fama • Burton Malkiel • Michael Jensen
John Maynard Keynes • George Akerlof • Robert Shiller • Richard Thaler

Suppose you have $100,000 to invest in equities. Should you take the advice of a financial analyst or trust your own judgment in picking the best shares? Can we really beat the market by listening to the advice of an economist? Some economists who have implicit faith in the efficiency of markets would humbly proclaim you're wasting your time, as beating the market is a fool's game. However, there are plenty of professionals who are much less modest and advise that just a few insights can give a competitive advantage.

Everybody likes to think they can beat the market. In fact, the psychologists **Daniel Kahneman** and **Amos Tversky** argue that overconfidence in our abilities is an intrinsic feature of human nature.

When it comes to selecting shares, a part of us feels in control and assumes we must be able to beat the market. But, alas, the reality is different. In the 2006 survey "Behaving Badly", James Montier found that 74% of professional fund managers who were surveyed believed they had above-average job performance, 26% viewed themselves as average and 0% considered themselves "below average"! This illusory superiority (as it is sometimes termed) does confirm the idea of optimism bias (*see* page 53).

The market (supposedly) can't be wrong...

If you still think you might have capacity to pick a winning share, there is a whole body of economic theory ready to squash your enthusiasm, in the form of the *efficient market hypothesis*. This theory was developed in the 1960s by the American economist and Nobel Laureate **Eugene Fama** (b. 1939), with the name coined by Harry Roberts in 1967. The basic idea is that in financial markets with many buyers and sellers, the price of a security accurately reflects a fair market price given the information available. If a stock were seriously undervalued compared with its fair value, there would be enough investors who would start buying to push it up to its long-term average. In other words, the

> *"Overconfidence arises because people are often blind to their own blindness"*
> Daniel Kahneman

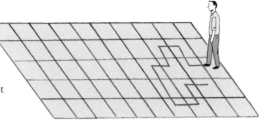

market can't be wrong, so don't bother trying to beat it.

Andrew Smithers, a British economist who has written about stock market bubbles, notes, "The Efficient Market Hypothesis says something extremely simple, which is that shares are always correctly priced".

The implication of the efficient market hypothesis is that the movement of share prices is like a random walk. This concept was popularized by the American economist and writer **Burton Malkiel** (b. 1932) in his 1973 book *A Random Walk Down Wall Street*. It suggests that if you want to pick a share, you might as well simply flip a coin.

Even better, choose a low-cost broker and buy into the average of the stock market (such as an *index fund*). According to Malkiel, the key is to buy an index of equities and hold on for the long term. The best strategy is not to look at the cyclical ups and downs, which may spook you into selling, but just buy and hold on for several years. Malkiel is particularly critical of *chartist* strategies (looking for trends in share prices), which, although appealing to people seeking order within markets, have little bearing in reality.

In 1978, the American financial economist **Michael Jensen** (b. 1939) wrote, "I believe there is no other proposition in economics which has more solid empirical evidence supporting it than the efficient market hypothesis." But if you're not convinced by the theory of efficient markets and a random walk, there are other economists and analysts willing to offer very different advice.

Random walk theory where share prices evolve according to random, unexpected patterns.

...or can it?

John Maynard Keynes (who once claimed he had made three fortunes on the stock market and lost two) noted a surprising result from studying share prices. He found that companies who made ice had a share price that did better in summer. This anecdotal evidence seems to challenge the efficient market hypothesis because the annual arrival of summer is not unknown knowledge. If you want to beat the market, buy ice-cream shares in May and sell in October. Supporters of the efficient market hypothesis will suggest it is just a coincidence – an inevitable one if you cherry-pick results from history. But Keynes was unrepentant, arguing that there was plenty of opportunity to be smarter than the average investor, if you were willing to take a *contrarian* point of view (doing the opposite of what others are doing).

Behavioural economists have argued that the efficient market hypothesis misunderstands human nature and ignores people's capacity for irrational decision-making. If we can understand this behavioural theory, it opens up the possibility of seeing options the market overlooks.

The economists **George Akerlof** and **Robert Shiller** (b. 1946) argue in their 2009 book *Animal Spirits* that investors make decisions based on emotion and the exuberance of crowds, rather than making rational choices that reflect the real value of the investment. The stock market bubble and crash of 1987 show the ability for financial investors to lose perspective. To beat the market, behavioural economists state that you have to be willing to go against the herd behaviour of the crowd.

Economic theory:
The efficient market hypothesis suggests share prices will be correctly valued, therefore picking a winner is only down to good luck.

Finding a bargain

Amos Tversky and **Richard Thaler** argue that a feature of private investment is *myopic loss aversion*, which means we have greater sensitivity to losses than to gains. As a result, most investors overvalue low-risk, low-return assets such as government bonds or blue chip companies. The way to beat the market, therefore, is to investigate small, undervalued companies with potential for growth. Thaler argues that one of the best guides for choosing stocks and shares is the simple, old-fashioned *price-to-earnings ratio* (which are used to evaluate companies' stock prices). Stocks that have a low price-to-earnings ratio are relatively cheap and offer more potential for growth than overvalued shares or bonds with poor returns. The important thing is not to get spooked by day-to-day share volatility.

In a market of innumerable investors, it is unsurprising that there are some who have a track record of beating the market. The philosophy of the high-profile investor Peter Lynch is to research companies where he might have a competitive advantage

How do I beat the market?

☐ Find information that others don't have

☐ Identify irrational behaviour of markets

☐ Get lucky

☐ Choose good value stocks that others wrongly think are risky

> *"The market can remain irrational*
> *longer than you can remain solvent"*
> John Maynard Keynes

over city brokers. Contrary to the efficient market hypothesis, Lynch argues that market information is *not* perfect. Brokers in New York don't go to visit small companies in Illinois to find their real value. Therefore, if you spend a lot of time researching local companies, you can find some that are currently mispriced by the market. It simply requires hard work and a willingness to avoid the exuberance of market fluctuations and stick to companies with good value. If you don't have time to visit companies, at least scrutinize their balance sheets.

Warren Buffett, the famous investment strategist, offers simple advice to maximize returns from the stock market. He recommends advising short-term fluctuations, buying low-cost Standard & Poor (S&P) 500 Index funds and staying in for the long term. Buffet argues that private investors often end up losing out because they spend a lot of money on expensive,

esoteric-sounding advice. The problem is that investment analysts have a vested interest in complicating investment – thereby encouraging reasons for buying and selling, and then charging a lot of money for this. Buffett suggests that the problem with professional advice is that they are trying to beat each other. But your chances of beating the market are 50% – or actually less when you consider transaction costs. The plethora of financial advisers promising to beat the market can't *all* be right.

But can you really beat the market? Even behavioural economists like Kahneman are dubious. He has little faith in private investors beating the market. Even knowing that shares are overvalued is no guarantee for making money. In 1997, internet stocks were already overvalued, but betting against internet stocks would have lost a lot of money between 1997 and 1999, when the bubble finally burst.

Making a decision:
If you agree with the efficient market hypothesis of Fama, you would be better off buying low-cost index funds. However, if you agree with Thaler that emotion drives buying and selling, you may be able to avoid market spirit and try to pick seemingly high-risk stocks with the potential to outperform the markets.

How do I survive inflation?

John Maynard Keynes • Irving Fisher • Martin Feldstein • Lionel Robbins
Jeremy Bulow • John B Shoven • Milton Friedman • Alan Blinder
Ludwig von Mises • Roy Jastram • Claude B Erb • Paul Krugman

Inflation is a continued increase in the price level and a rise in the cost of living. For individuals it means rising prices and a likely decline in the value of savings. Economists from David Ricardo to Milton Friedman agree that inflation imposes a severe cost on both individuals and economies – but what advice, if any, can economists give for dealing with the reality of inflation?

Contrary to popular opinion, **John Maynard Keynes** wrote extensively about the dangers of inflation. He claimed that inflation is effectively a form of tax on the original holders of banknotes. In other words, if you have significant cash reserves, inflation will steadily reduce the value of your money. An annual inflation rate of 10% means the cash under your mattress will buy 10% fewer goods in 12 months' time. Given the way inflation eats away at the real value of your savings, the first response to inflation is to try to protect your savings' value by putting your money in assets, such as housing, shares or commodities, which will hopefully increase in line with inflation and protect the purchasing power of your wealth.

Irving Fisher, a contemporary of Keynes, developed a simple equation (known as the *Fisher equation*). It states that the real interest rate equals the nominal interest rate minus inflation. The importance of this is that if nominal interest rates are higher than inflation, then keeping money in a bank account will protect its value. For example, if the nominal interest rate is 8% and inflation is 5%, then the real interest rate is 3% and money held in that account will actually gain in value. In this situation, the incentive is to keep cash in your bank account rather than loose cash.

If you can get a positive (i.e., greater than zero) real interest rate, then your savings will be protected, but this is not always the case. During the prolonged economic downturn and liquidity trap of 2009–16, in many Western economies interest rates were 0.5%, but inflation spiked to 3–5%. In this situation, inflation will make savers worse off.

The Fisher equation

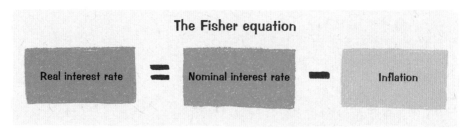

Real interest rate = Nominal interest rate − Inflation

> *"By a continuing process of inflation, governments can confiscate, secretly and unobserved, an important part of the wealth of their citizens"*
> John Maynard Keynes

The usual advice to counter this is to invest in assets – real estate, shares, bonds and gold. American economist **Martin Feldstein** (b. 1939) investigated the effects of inflation in the US and found that it discouraged saving but encouraged activity in the housing market. House prices tend to rise during periods of inflation and provide an intrinsic store of wealth. Furthermore, if you borrow (getting a mortgage) to buy a house, inflation will help reduce the real value of your mortgage debt – inflation can reward borrowers.

Dealing with hyperinflation

If inflation of 3–5% tends to be relatively manageable, what about inflation rates of more than 20–40%, as we have seen in emerging economies such as those of Argentina and Russia? In writing about the costs of Argentina, Feldstein comments that high inflation wiped out the market for life insurance, as future payouts could not be guaranteed. He notes that high inflation encourages people to hold savings in foreign currency with a history of lower inflation (such as the US dollar). But if capital controls prevent people from buying foreign currency, they need to find more creative ways to protect their wealth. In Argentina, for example, instead of putting money in a bank, people can make several payments toward the purchase of a new car. Although the car loses 20% of its value after purchase, it holds its value better than savings in Argentinian banks.

Argentina has seen inflation of 40%, but how do you survive hyperinflation rates, which we occasionally see, for example in Zimbabwe (2000s) and Germany (1923)? Keynes and Fisher would have been well aware of the destructive costs of hyperinflation in Germany. One apocryphal story recounts how a journalist went into a coffee shop and looked at the menu, on which a coffee cost 5,000 marks. When he finished drinking two cups an hour later, the waiter presented a bill for 14,000 marks. The journalist hadn't looked at the menu before ordering the second one and during the time it took to drink the coffees, the price had shot up! In this extreme situation of hyperinflation, you learn to spend as soon as you get paid.

Economists such as **Lionel Robbins** (1898–1984) who studied Germany's hyperinflation of 1923 found that inflation wiped away many savings accounts. When teachers got paid at 10.00am, relatives would come into school and go and spend the wages because they wouldn't be able to buy anything by the end of the day. Robbins notes that the only group who prospered from high inflation were those who owned physical assets and physical capital, such as industrialists who owned factories. If firms are raising prices faster than wages, it is an opportunity for them to increase profit. Therefore, in periods of inflation, buying shares can be an effective way to hold on to wealth.

Jeremy Bulow (b. 1954), in a paper with **John B Shoven** (b. 1947), noted that inflation can often lead to rising company profits because high inflation reduces the real value of debt and hence the borrowing costs of firms effectively fall. And as Robbins notes, even during the German hyperinflation of 1923, share prices matched the inflation rate and even exceeded it. Shares were a good investment during German hyperinflation.

However, other economists, such as **Milton Friedman**, caution that although inflation may temporarily boost profits, in the long run it damages economic activity through creating uncertainty and discouraging long-term investment. Therefore, Friedman would be more cautious about investing in the stock market in periods of high inflation.

Also, it does depend on the type of inflation. The American economist **Alan Blinder** (b. 1945) noted that the global inflation of the 1970s was primarily caused by *cost-push factors* (issues that cause an increase in firms' costs, such as rising prices of raw materials and energy, and wage costs). In this case firms will not benefit from rising prices as costs may be rising faster than the prices they can charge.

Economic theory:
Inflation reduces the real value of money. Therefore, savers will have to ensure they maintain a positive real interest rate or find an alternative form of investment such as gold or equities.

Gold as a hedge against inflation

Gold is often held up as a good hedge against inflation. **Ludwig von Mises** was a prominent adherent of the *Austrian school* of economics (which generally supports laissez-faire economics – absence of government intervention – and argues that a major cause of inflation is when interest rates that are set too low cause a credit bubble and rise in money supply). Von Mises advocated a return to the gold standard because gold avoided the costs of inflation associated with *fiat* (paper) currency. He noted that gold has an intrinsic wealth and has a long history of being used as an accepted means

"The return to gold does not depend on the fulfilment of some material condition. It is an ideological problem. It presupposes only one thing: the abandonment of the illusion that increasing the quantity of money creates prosperity"
Ludwig von Mises

of exchange; furthermore it has a strong emotional significance as a symbol of wealth and security. Given the fact that modern fiat currencies are subject to the prospect of inflation, analysts sympathetic to Austrian economics frequently advise purchasing gold as a means to store your wealth and avoid the debasement of the currency. The logic is that a government can always print more money, but it can't print more gold.

However, **Roy Jastram** (1915–91), author of the influential 1977 book *The Golden Constant*, notes that gold has historically been a poor hedge against inflation in the short run. It does tend to hold its value in the long run, but the long run may mean a hundred years! And while gold holds its value, it offers no interest and is usually outperformed by equities. **Claude B Erb**, co-author of *The Golden Dilemma* (2012), makes a similar observation about investing in gold. He noted that between 1980 and 2000, when Brazil had an inflation rate of 100%, holding cash would have led to a 100% decline in cash savings. But because of the global fall in the price of gold during that period,

During hyperinflation try converting money into assets (if you can).

holding gold would still have led to a 70% decline in your savings. In other words, gold is no guaranteed hedge against inflation.

The role of expectations

Milton Friedman investigated how the impact of inflation can depend on how it behaves compared with expectations. In essence, if inflation is higher than you expect, it tends to cost savers. In the US in the early 1970s, if you expected low inflation of, say, 4%, you would be happy to buy a government bond at an interest rate of 6%, giving a real rate of return of 2%. Unfortunately, in that period, inflation turned out to be much higher than most expected. With inflation running at 10–20%, people who bought bonds saw a fall in the real value of them. The problem is that it is no easy matter to start predicting future inflation. Friedman would advise looking at whether the government is running large budget deficits and is willing to increase the money supply – if so, this is likely to be inflationary, and it would be better to buy index-linked bonds (bonds automatically linked to inflation).

However, even a knowledge of *monetarist theory* – which holds that the main way to stabilize the economy is by controlling the *money supply* (the amount of money in circulation) – is no guide to how inflation will behave. In 2008–9, high oil prices led to a temporary jump in the inflation rate. But the recession caused the US and UK governments to create money through the policy of quantitative easing. How to react

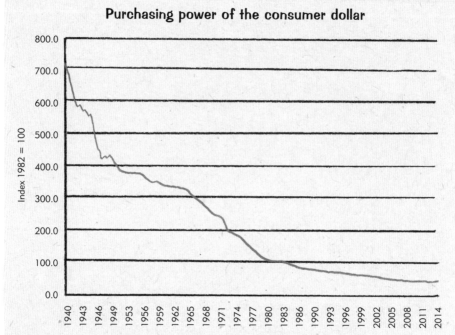

Purchasing power of the consumer dollar

Index 1982 = 100

800.0
700.0
600.0
500.0
400.0
300.0
200.0
100.0
0.0

1940 1943 1946 1949 1953 1956 1959 1962 1965 1968 1971 1974 1977 1980 1983 1986 1990 1993 1996 1999 2002 2005 2008 2011 2014

How inflation has eroded the value of money – meaning one dollar can purchase fewer goods.

to this unwelcome combination of inflation and recession? Using monetarist models, some investors predicted high inflation and advised buying gold. But despite a tripling in the monetary base, inflation never materialized. Furthermore, between 2012 and 2016 the gold price fell.

The American economist and journalist **Paul Krugman** (b. 1953) has been critical of those who have exaggerated the fear of inflation in the 2010s. He explains that in a *depressed economy* (with falling GDP/output) and *liquidity trap* (when interest rates are close to zero), increasing the money supply is very unlikely to cause inflation. Inflation can be very costly for savers, but in a liquidity trap, Krugman advises not succumbing to excess fears.

Making a decision:

In a period of inflation, von Mises may advise holding gold as an inflation-proof investment. However, other economists such as Feldstein suggest you will get a better return from purchasing equities or real estate.

How can I make my small business more profitable?

Joseph Schumpeter • Peter F Drucker • Dan Ariely • Albert O Hirschman • Steven Horwitz • William Stanley Jevons • Alfred Marshall • Richard Thaler • Tim Harford

It is a real challenge to keep a small business afloat – an estimated 50% of small firms fail in the first year. If your small business is facing a decline in profit or even closure, can traditional theory and insights from behavioural economics offer any practical advice for turning around your business and increasing profitability?

The Austrian-born American economist **Joseph Schumpeter** (1883–1950) developed an influential concept entitled *creative destruction*, which observed how, in a capitalist economy, markets are continuously changing.

The implication is that businesses can never rest on their laurels. Markets, technology and consumer preferences can change so quickly that formerly successful businesses can soon get left behind. Any failure to adapt and keep up with trends means businesses can quickly become unprofitable. Schumpeter saw the "destructive process" as a positive engine of growth. But for a business to stay profitable, it involves a willingness to make continuous change – such as replacing workers with automated technology or offering new lines of products. Small firms who can't keep up with the latest mobile technology could soon see themselves swamped. Similarly, **Peter F Drucker** (1909–2005), an Austrian-born American management consultant, argued that an attachment to the old way of doing things can be a major stumbling block for small businesses.

A difficulty that a business may have is an emotional attachment to unprofitable workers or to the way things have been done in the past. This is why it can be useful to bring in an outside consultant, who can advocate radical change unencumbered by attachments. The lesson from Schumpeter is that you have to ride the wave of creative destruction, staying on the right side of change.

Improving workers' motivation and spotting problems

However, while a radical approach to restructuring may be helpful at certain times, the behavioural economist **Dan Ariely** claims that a successful business needs to be able to motivate workers – not through threats of redundancy but by fostering a sense of responsibility, trust and pride in their work. The good news is that you don't necessarily have to give big bonuses. Ariely believes that financial motivation is only a very limited motivating factor, and financial bonuses may be not only unnecessary but also counterproductive. Even the simple act of offering appreciation can do wonders for staff morale and business profitability.

In contrast to Schumpeter, the German-born American economist **Albert O Hirschman** (1915–2012) is more suspicious of the creative destructive process. Whereas Schumpeter suggests that firms will feel the winds of changing preferences, Hirschman argues that companies can easily miss important signals. He argues that consumers use two main strategies – *voice* and *exit*. If people are dissatisfied with a monopoly company, they may complain because there is no alternative. However, complaining requires effort and cost; most consumers prefer simply to exit and quietly move elsewhere. The implication for business in competitive markets is that they could be losing their customer base, without being conscious of why.

It is said that for every customer who complains to business owners, another 99 silently exit the firm and perhaps complain to their friends. Hirschman argues that the secret of good business is the willingness to spot potential problems and act on them. This may require a proactive strategy through questionnaires, secret shoppers, outside consultants and, above all, a willingness to hear and respond to negative feedback. The main lesson is not to leave it too late.

Economic theory:
Lessons from behavioural economics suggest that small changes such as harnessing default options can help increase profitability.

Making decisions at the margin

The American economist **Steven Horwitz** (b. 1964) notes that business can be susceptible to the *sunk cost fallacy*. A sunk cost is an investment we cannot recover. For example, we have a great idea to spend $10,000 on a fancy IT upgrade. But, we soon realize it doesn't work and is causing more problems than it solves. However, because we've spent $10,000, we kill ourselves trying to make it work, to justify all that outlay – but this only causes more losses for the business. A more logical way is to ignore this sunk cost, write off the expensive mistake and outsource the issue to a company that can do it more efficiently. In everyday terms, we may talk about "cutting our losses", but the principle

"…incessantly destroying the old one, incessantly creating a new one. This process of Creative Destruction is the essential fact about capitalism"
Joseph Schumpeter

40% off → Discount upfront ticket =
• Increased revenue
• Higher profits
• Better cash flow
• Happier customers

is the same: don't worry about the past but make decisions at the margin (i.e., look at the costs and benefits of your next action). It comes back to the work of **William Stanley Jevons**: ignore total costs, but examine the marginal benefits and marginal costs (*see* page 19) of continuing with a business decision.

The simplest way to increase profits is to increase price. However, an important concept in economics developed by **Alfred Marshall** is that of *elasticity* – if price increases, how much does demand change? If your business has many close substitutes, consumers are more likely to be price sensitive. Therefore price rises may lead to lower revenue. However, if demand is inelastic – through brand differentiation – consumers will be willing to pay higher prices. If you know whether your demand is price elastic or price inelastic, it can help your price strategy.

Insights from behavioural economics

The owner of a small business could learn much from the relatively new discipline of behavioural economics. In *Misbehaving: the Making of Behavioural Economics*, **Richard Thaler** was asked to give business advice to a ski resort struggling to stay afloat. He advised making use of mental accounting (*see* page 33) to help increase prices without making consumers feel they were being ripped off. The resort used to charge a single price per visit. Thaler suggested selling in advance season tickets of ten visits with 40% off the usual price. Consumers feel they are getting a bargain – there is a positive transaction utility (*see* page 73). The ski resort gets more money upfront (good for cash flow at the start of the season). But, importantly, total revenue increases because, in practice, most people don't use all ten tickets. Here the secret is giving a deal to consumers that gives them a feeling of getting a bargain, but ends up with more revenue for your firm.

Another concept is *price targeting* – how do you get wealthy consumers to pay more without alienating cost-conscious consumers? In the book *The Undercover Economist*, the British economist and journalist **Tim Harford** looked at why some

> *"If they could charge a high price to the lavish (or concerned) and a low price to the thrifty (or unconcerned) then they could enjoy the best of both worlds"*
> Tim Harford

coffee shops sell fair trade coffee at a premium even though the cost difference is very minor. The reason is that fair trade coffee is a way of charging a higher price to those willing to pay for it. By contrast, those who are price conscious are happy to get the cheaper coffee from the menu. This principle of price targeting can be applied to many different businesses – for example, those offering organic options or premium service.

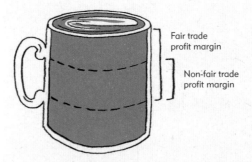

Charging a higher price for fair trade coffee enables firms to target consumers willing to pay more.

Sometimes, even small things can make a big difference. Richard Thaler notes the power of the *default choice*. To sign up for a service, firms make it really easy, but if you want to cancel a subscription, a lot more effort is required. The business journal *McKinsey Quarterly* noted how an Italian telephone company made subtle changes to discourage people quitting their service.

Initially, if consumers kept their plan, they would be offered 100 free calls. This was changed to "We have already credited your account with 100 calls – how could you use those?" which led to a big drop in cancellations. It is an example of the endowment theory (*see* page 25). If we are told that we already have 100 calls in our account, we don't want to cancel as we will lose what we already have, whereas with the previous approach we don't feel the same attachment to calls that we don't yet own.

Making a decision:

Reading Harford and Thaler, you might like to apply insights from behavioural economics to find ways to nudge consumers into spending more. Or you may agree with Hirschman that the most important thing is to seek customer feedback to check whether you are making any fundamental mistakes and getting left behind. However, Ariely suggests the fundamental problem may just be finding the right way to motivate your workers.

How much should I put into retirement savings?

Alfred Marshall • John Maynard Keynes • Franco Modigliani • Mervyn King
Hersh Shefrin • Richard Thaler • Daniel Kahneman • Amos Tversky
Shlomo Benartzi • Laurence Kotlikoff • Andy Haldane

We are constantly been told to save more for our retirement. Yet, faced with pressing bills and other priorities, there is a temptation to delay saving and make the most of the present moment. However, while some people fail to save enough for retirement, there are also economists who warn about pressures from the finance industry to make us save too much.

Early classical economists, such as **Alfred Marshall**, saw saving as a virtue. It partly reflected the Victorian concepts of thrift, hard work and prudence, but also, in an era when government support for old age was either nonexistent or patchy, saving was essential to provide some security in old age. (It is interesting to note that Alfred Marshall also cautioned about misers, whose "passion for saving borders on insanity".)

John Maynard Keynes is often seen as the first economist to challenge the virtue of saving – however, this is not quite correct. Keynes simultaneously saw saving as a private virtue and as a potential problem for the macroeconomy. His concern is known as the *paradox of thrift* – if everyone saves more in a recession, it causes a further fall in aggregate demand. But this issue makes no difference to your optimal level of saving for retirement.

Smoothing consumption

The Italian–American economist and Nobel Laureate **Franco Modigliani** (1918–2003) developed what is known as the *life-cycle hypothesis*. This is an understanding that rational individuals attempt to smooth (even out) their consumption over a lifetime. In other words, during our working life, we save a percentage of income toward our retirement, at which time we can draw down our savings. The basic principle is that we gain increased utility by saving for retirement rather than spending everything now. It goes back to the principle of diminishing marginal utility of money (*see* page 21). If we spend all our income when young, we gain little extra satisfaction, and we may then suffer privation when we are old and unable to work. Modigliani's theory states that we should make use of our earning power when working, in order to save for a decent pension in retirement.

In a study of saving, the British economist and former governor of the Bank of England **Mervyn King** (b. 1948) found that the life-cycle hypothesis reflected the broad attitude of the population to saving, but was inadequate for a minority of the population who ignore the importance of saving for

> *"Economics has an enormous amount to offer the financial planning industry. But the industry has ignored economics, providing millions of Americans with what I and other economists view as truly awful advice"*
> Laurence Kotlikoff

a pension. This is echoed in statistics that suggest that, in 2016, one-third of Americans had zero retirement savings.

The power of the present

Why do we find it so difficult to save for the future, when economic theory suggests it is the rational thing to do? The behavioural economists **Hersh Shefrin** (b. 1948) and **Richard Thaler** talk about a kind of split personality within a person. They argue that there is a higher self concerned with long-term consequences and a lower self concerned with immediate pleasure. When making decisions about saving, we face a dilemma between these two opposites, and it can lead to under-saving.

In a similar vein, economists such as Ted O'Donoghue have noted the importance of a present bias (*see* page 21) in our decisions, which means that many of us place greater value on money now compared with money in the future. The further in the future it is, the less we value it. This can explain why long-term pension consequences can get swamped by concerns about short-term needs and wants. When the present bias is strong, we under-save for our retirement.

Daniel Kahneman and **Amos Tversky** also considered the difficulty people face in dealing with decisions involving uncertainty. Given the complexity of pensions and the innumerable choices to be made,

people often devise simple rules of thumb that are not based on rational smoothing consumption over a life cycle. In practice it can lead to procrastination where, even though we think our savings are too low, we put off unappealing decisions like committing to a pension plan. Life-cycle theories assume rationality, but in reality procrastination and deferment are powerful elements of human nature and can easily lead to our saving less than an optimal amount.

To overcome this status quo bias, or preference for the present state of affairs (*see* page 81), Richard Thaler and **Shlomo Benartzi** (b. 1968) developed a new pension program called "Save More Tomorrow" (or SMarT). The premise is that workers commit to save into a pension – but only pay in the contribution when they get a pay rise in the future. The advantage is that we feel like

Economic theory:
The life-cycle hypothesis suggests we should save enough during our working life to be able to fund a similar level of consumption during retirement.

137

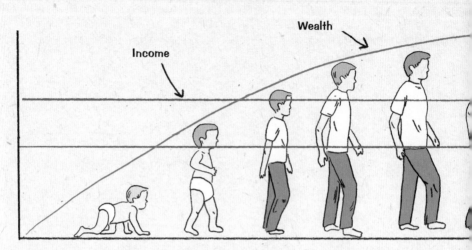

During our working life we save for retirement, then we run down these savings to enable stable consumption throughout our life.

we are not losing out, and we don't sacrifice any of our current salary, but only pay future rises toward a pension. The other advantage is that once committed to the plan, we automatically pay toward a pension unless we opt out – it becomes the default option, not requiring any effort on our part. Take-up rates for SMarT pension plans have been high and drop-out rates low. It suggests that, left to our own devices, we may under-save, but if we are given an attractive saving plan that addresses issues of our loss aversion (*see* page 41) and our procrastination, we can find saving for a pension more attractive.

Over-saving

While many of us may under-save toward a pension, the American economist **Laurence Kotlikoff** (b. 1951) argues that individuals should be cautious about accepting the conventional wisdom of the pensions industry. He argues that rules of thumb about the percentage of income you need to save for a pension are often exaggerated, because pension funds have a vested interest in getting you to save more than you really need to. He claims that income replacement rates of 70–85% of final income (your salary in your last year of employment) will often prove more than you will be able to spend.

Rather than worry about retirement, a young person should be aware that the early part of their life has much higher costs, such as buying a house and bringing up children, all of which will be considerably lower in retirement. Also, travelling the world is easier when you are young and mobile, rather than old and tired. As well as smoothing income

"The man who dies rich, dies disgraced"
Andrew Carnegie

Retirement

Consumption

over a life cycle, we should also consider smoothing our leisure time. Is it worth working a stressful 50-hour week to get a big pension in 40 years' time?

Andy Haldane (b. 1967), a chief economist at the Bank of England, concurs. He admits that he finds pensions remarkably confusing, and he argues that property is better at funding a retirement than a pension is. Property values have increased in value, and if a mortgage is paid off, it will reduce living costs compared with having to pay rent into old age.

Another issue with the life-cycle hypothesis is that it assumes we will run down our savings in old age, but usually this doesn't occur. People become attached to wealth and savings and desire to pass it on to their children.

However, if we are leaving large sums, it may suggest that Kotlikoff is correct in suggesting that many of us are over-saving. The billionaire industrialist Andrew Carnegie argued that if we accumulate wealth and fail to spend it, we will just spoil our children.

Making a decision:

You may agree with Thaler that you are procrastinating and are saving an insufficient amount toward your pension. In that case, look for a way to make it easier to save, such as a pension plan that overcomes your inertia. However, you may prefer to follow the advice of Kotlikoff and save only a moderate amount so that you can get the most out of life while you are still young enough to enjoy it.

How do I avoid getting caught by financial bubbles?

Carmen Reinhart • Kenneth Rogoff • Hyman Minsky • Irving Fisher
Alan Greenspan • Robert Shiller • Karl Case

Financial bubbles occur when there is a rapid increase in the value of an asset, before a dramatic fall in value. Over the centuries, some of the most dramatic have included the South Sea Bubble of 1720, the 1929 Wall Street Crash and the dot-com bubble of the late 1990s. A feature of financial bubbles is that it is very easy to be wise after the event, yet despite many high-profile cases, burst bubbles still catch out many investors (and famous economists). Can economic theory offer us any insights into spotting and avoiding bubbles?

In their 2009 book *This Time is Different*, **Carmen Reinhart** (b. 1955) and **Kenneth Rogoff** (b. 1953) investigated major financial bubbles of the past eight centuries, including Tulip Mania in 1637 and the credit crunch of 2007–8, and found many recurring aspects. One feature was that otherwise intelligent people would feel, in their particular case, that different rules of valuation were applying. In other words, people felt there was some specific, extenuating reason for the asset to increase far beyond its usual valuation.

Don't follow the herd

The enthusiasm of the market is infectious, and consciously or unconsciously we start to follow "the wisdom of the crowds". This is often referred to as *herd behaviour* or *herd instinct*, because it is easier to follow the majority. We doubt ourselves because we wonder how we could be right and everyone else wrong. But successful investors like Warren Buffett argue that a *contrarian* attitude (*see* page 123) is necessary to be able to beat the market.

Approaching the tipping point

The American economist **Hyman Minsky** (1919–96) studied financial markets and made investigations into financial bubbles. In particular, he argued that in periods of economic prosperity, banks and individuals tend to expand credit at a faster rate than economic growth. The good economic news and high confidence encourage a growth of credit and an increase in the value of assets

> *"Be fearful when others are greedy, and greedy when others are fearful"*
> Warren Buffett

The Minsky moment

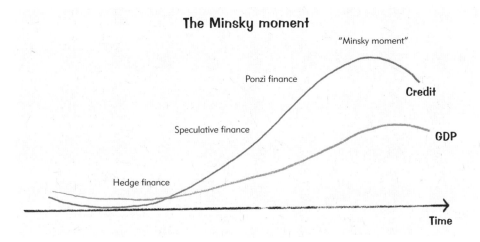

that is greater than their underlying value. In other words, stability itself leads to instability.

However, when the economy dips, banks wish to call in their loans, and the availability of credit can fall sharply. This tipping point, where we go from credit expansion to credit contraction, has been dubbed the *Minsky moment* – and it is this that causes bubbles to burst. For many years, Minsky's *financial instability hypothesis*, as these theories were called, was largely fringe in the economics profession. A more dominant theory was the efficient market hypothesis (*see* page 122), the idea that markets reflected the real value of an asset based on available information. But, the credit crunch of 2007–8 led to a resurgence of interest in Minsky's theories.

The practical application of Minsky's theories is to look at underlying value rather than the momentum of the market. If you examine share prices of internet companies in the 1990s, they were trading on previously unheard-of price-to-earnings ratios (*see* page 124). Even companies who were yet to make a profit were surging in value. The logic of the market in the late 1990s was "this time is different" because the internet was something new. But, right on cue, the dot-com bubble burst. This time really wasn't any different.

Crystal ball gazing

Minsky's work built upon previous theories of the American neoclassical economist **Irving Fisher.** Fisher developed a theory about credit bubbles and the dynamics of *debt deflation* (a period of falling prices, causing the real burden of debt to increase) to explain the stock market crash and prolonged Great Depression. While his work on debt deflation was later widely admired, his ability to predict the bursting of a bubble was, unfortunately, less prescient. Just nine days before the 29 October 1929 Wall Street Crash, Fisher confidently predicted that prices had "reached what looks like a permanently high plateau". He then spent the next few months saying that share prices would soon recover as the prices hadn't reached their true value. As a result, he lost both a financial fortune and his academic reputation. It was perhaps bad luck, and it should be noted that he wasn't the only

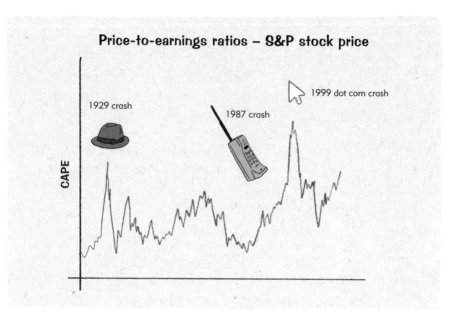

Price-to-earnings ratios – S&P stock price

1929 crash

1987 crash

1999 dot com crash

CAPE

economist to lose his shirt on the stock
market. John Maynard Keynes also incurred
significant losses after the Wall Street Crash
of 1929.

Rational investment

At this point, a good question to ask is, why
don't we learn from past mistakes concerning
credit and asset bubbles? Why do we keep
falling for bubbles?

In 1996, the then-chairman of America's
Federal Reserve, **Alan Greenspan**
(b. 1926), gave a speech in which he
warned of "irrational exuberance".
Greenspan warned investors about getting
carried away by market sentiment and the
enthusiasm of investors, which becomes
divorced from the underlying value of assets.
The irony of Greenspan's comment is that
he has often been criticized for not doing
more to prevent the bubbles of the late
1990s and 2000-7.

The American economist **Robert Shiller**
challenged the dominant view that stock
markets tend to reflect a fair value (the
efficient market hypothesis – *see* above and
page 122). Asking investors what motivated
them to buy assets, he found that it was
often emotional reasons rather than the
rational evaluation of value. Because of
the herd behaviour of investors, assets could
become divorced from value. Shiller argued
that a rational investor should value a share
according to expected future dividends
discounted for the present time. This led
him to predict that the stock market was
overvalued in 2000 and 2007. He used the
same analysis for the US housing market.

Shiller's work is not without its limitations;
looking at the price-to-earnings ratio is
not enough to predict future stock market
trends. For example, in the US in 1949–55
there was a strong *bull market* (when share
prices are rising); the *Dow Jones Industrial*

Average (a stock market index) tripled in seven years, from 161 to 487. There was a rise in price-to-earnings ratios but there was no crash – the rise was sustainable. Even in 1929, share prices were not as wildly overvalued as we might expect. The Cyclically Adjusted Price-to-Earnings ratio (CAPE) was 32 – high but not indicative of the huge falls to come (which is why Irving Fisher had thought prices would recover). The 90% fall in US share prices between 1929 and 1932 was due not just to overvalued shares but to the collapse in the real economy and earnings.

Shiller, with **Karl Case** (1946–2016), developed the *Case–Shiller home price index*, arguing that, over the long term, US house prices tend to return to the real values of 1890 (which is how far back in time the index was calculated). In other words, when real house prices rise faster than earnings, this tends to be unsustainable, leading to a future correction. In 2005, when many real estate investors were predicting further rises in house prices, Shiller foresaw a major house price fall by 2006 or 2007. His strategy of

Economic theory:

Markets are subject to irrational exuberance and overconfidence, therefore an investor should ignore conventional wisdom but examine fair value.

relying on the underlying real values proved effective in forecasting the housing bubble. The US housing bubble burst, as did similar housing bubbles in Europe, especially in countries like Spain and Ireland.

Shiller offers investors important lessons. Don't be caught up in the irrational exuberance of the time. In particular, be wary when people tell you "this time it is different". If you want to develop the capacity to spot bubbles, you need the confidence to ignore the prevailing market sentiment.

Making a decision:

You may agree with the efficient market hypothesis that you have no better chance of spotting a bubble than markets who have the same information as yourself. However, you could easily prefer the ideas of Minsky, who argues that markets frequently get it wrong or get carried away by excess enthusiasm, and that a better guide is to use long-term price-to-earnings valuations.

How much personal debt should I take on?

Adam Smith • David Ricardo • Max Weber • Thorstein Veblen • Ludwig von Mises
Dan Ariely • Paul Krugman • Milton Friedman • Ha-Joon Chang • David Graeber
Muhammad Yunus

Despite rising levels of GDP in recent decades, we have paradoxically seen a rapid increase in household debt. A mortgage to buy a house may seem prudent, but credit card debt to buy luxury goods is usually considered extravagant and is possibly damaging. What do economists say? Is this rise in debt a sign of economic progress or the road to personal ruin?

Classical economists (*see* page 10) such as **Adam Smith** and **David Ricardo** tended to take a dim view of debt in general, though they didn't write much about personal debt because it was less of an issue in their time. Attitudes toward personal debt were similar to the attitude toward government debt. This partly reflected the morality of going into debt – the fear that outstanding obligations could damage your character.

An influential book in this regard was *The Protestant Ethic and the Spirit of Capitalism* (1905) by **Max Weber.** He argued that the early success of capitalism stemmed from the Protestant ethic of hard work, frugality and modesty in worldly affairs. To Weber, the spirit of capitalism was a set of values that emphasized progress and sobriety. In this world of moral capitalism there is no room for *conspicuous consumption* (a term introduced by a contemporary of Weber, the economist **Thorstein Veblen,** to mean spending lavishly to impress the Joneses) financed by consumer credit. The Protestant work ethic prioritized saving over borrowing. Even a small debt was seen as potentially leading to personal misery.

The theme was taken up by **Ludwig von Mises**. In examining European society, von Mises was highly critical of his Austrian countrymen who seemed to have little concern for the future and didn't hesitate to add debt, in order to finance consumption. Von Mises felt that it wasn't just a question of morality. He blamed the financial crisis of 1912–13 on the liquidation of unsustainable borrowing systems of previous years.

Debt and human psychology

Von Mises noted that individuals and especially governments could be swept up in the emotion of the time and make very poor intertemporal decisions (decisions over time). In recent years, behavioural economists have suggested new concepts to explain how we can end up getting sucked into taking on too much personal debt. **Dan Ariely**, in his 2008 book *Predictably Irrational*, argues that, far from making rational decisions maximizing utility over time, we are driven by emotions. In particular, humans can be poor at abstract long-term planning and end up taking on too much debt. We are attracted by the

present consumption, which we value, but at a cost that is pushed into the future.

Companies can exploit our weakness in making long-term decisions, by pushing unsuitable loans. In explaining the run-up to the credit crunch of 2007–8, **Paul Krugman** and others noted how mortgage companies relaxed standards of lending, offering attractive "teaser" mortgage loans. These were specifically designed to offer low introductory rates, with higher long-term rates hidden in the small print. The period 2000–6 is a cautionary tale for borrowers. The economic myopia of borrowers desperate to get on the property ladder at a time of rising prices was combined with the predatory lending practices of unscrupulous mortgage companies, resulting in people taking on too much debt. The cost for borrowers was large-scale mortgage defaulting and home repossession. It is a similar story to the 1912–13 credit bubble that concerned von Mises.

How debt can help

Yet these credit bubbles are only part of the story of debt. A bigger component of personal debt is that it can help smooth our income over a lifetime.

Milton Friedman's *permanent income hypothesis* provides a more useful model for how debt can deal with fluctuations in income and maintain more consistent levels of spending. This model suggests that if we experience a temporary fall in income owing to, say, a recession, then it may be logical to take out a personal loan to maintain necessary spending and pay it back when the economy picks up. Similarly, taking on credit card debt in December can help smooth annual expenditure over the Christmas period. For the self-employed, debt can be a necessary way of maintaining cash flow when customers are late in paying or when investment is necessary. This model suggests debt has a clear economic rationale – borrowing to smooth out temporary drops in income.

With regard to personal debt, we should not be concerned as to whether it is a virtue or a vice, but whether it helps us. For example, the South Korean economist **Ha-Joon Chang** (b. 1963) makes the point that debt could be used as an investment in human capital (*see* page 86). If we take out a loan

"What can be added to the happiness of a man who is in health, out of debt, and has a clear conscience?"
Adam Smith

to enable us to attain a degree or technical qualification, then in the short term we are spending beyond our means, but our qualifications will enable us to earn a higher lifetime salary and pay back the loan.

We tend to think of debt/credit as a modern invention, but the anthropologist **David Graeber** (b. 1961) argues that debt agreements usually preceded both money and the system of bartering. Criticizing economic textbooks that assume money evolved from barter systems, he argues that debt agreements are a fundamental part of human nature and human society. Graeber points out that some of the earliest written human documents are Mesopotamian tablets recording credits and debits, such as money owed for rent of temple lands. He argues that early human societies used debt and gift exchanges as methods to cement local relationships, a system that worked quite well.

The wrong kind of debt?

Economists are not concerned about debt per se – but about the wrong kind of debt, such as loans with very high rates of interest, like *payday loans* (small, short-term loans). The economist Christine L Dobridge found that while payday credit could help families deal with periods of financial distress, easy access could create problems for households with strong preferences for current consumption and "self-control problems". Furthermore, payday loans can be seen as an exploitative form of credit, with annual interest rates of 500–900%. With these kinds of interest rates, small debts can easily snowball. For example, with an annualized rate of 390%, a $1,000 payday loan would cost $4,000 to repay if it was rolled over for a year.

Given that people who access payday loans tend to be poor, there is a popular distaste for those with very high interest rates. However,

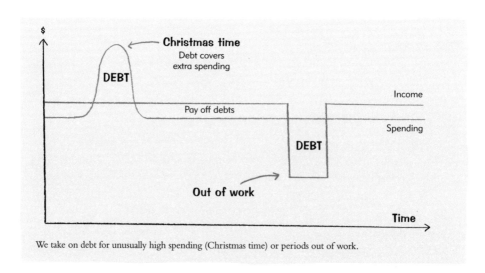

We take on debt for unusually high spending (Christmas time) or periods out of work.

Robert DeYoung challenges conventional wisdom and claims that payday loans can be a rational choice for those who find themselves in difficult situations. He argues that a payday loan can help avoid an even worse situation such as a parking ticket being escalated into a court order. DeYoung also points to surveys that suggest that many who take out payday loans correctly predict how long it will take them to pay it off. In other words, the over-optimism of borrowers feared by some behavioural economists may not be true. DeYoung argues that it is easy to criticize payday loans, when you don't face the circumstance that borrowers find themselves in.

While we often look upon debt as a problem, **Muhammad Yunus** (b. 1940), a Bangladeshi economist, banker, social entrepreneur and Nobel Laureate, has argued that greater extension of credit in the developing world is essential for unlocking human and social potential. Yunus argues that in the developing world, banks generally ignore the very poor (often women), leaving them stuck in very low-paid agricultural

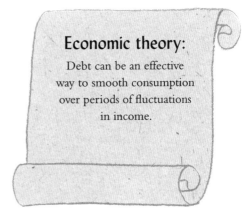

Economic theory:

Debt can be an effective way to smooth consumption over periods of fluctuations in income.

work. He sought to create "microbanks" which specifically made available small loans at low interest rates to these groups of people. Yunus claims that these loans had a very high rate of repayment and led to significant improvements in living standards as they enabled the poorest to invest in capital and higher productivity. He argues that extending credit at reasonable interest rates is more empowering than charity – because loans enable people to gain self-respect.

Making a decision:

If you have a temporary fall in income, you may agree with Friedman that it is rational to borrow to maintain basic income. However, Shiller would advise you to be careful of getting carried away by borrowing too much during an economic boom. Also, if you are borrowing to invest, you may agree with Yunus and Chang that debt can unlock some of your potential.

Politics

Page 150: Should I vote for a political party that promises to cut my income taxes?

Page 154: Should I boycott goods made in sweatshop factories?

Page 158: Should I support government subsidies for a local firm facing bankruptcy?

Page 162: Will I be better off with tariffs on imports?

Page 165: Should I welcome parking charges in my street and city?

Page 169: Should I support the legalization of drugs?

Page 173: Should I worry about my government getting into debt?

Page 177: Should we worry about rising inequality?

Page 180: Should health care be private or public?

Chapter 5

Should I vote for a political party that promises to cut my income taxes?

Greg Mankiw • Arthur Laffer • Friedrich Hayek • Paul Krugman
Milton Friedman • Paul Samuelson • Joseph Stiglitz

Lower income tax is popular for obvious reasons: you get to keep more of your hard-earned income. Furthermore, tax cuts can boost economic growth, provide incentives for more investment and encourage people to work harder. However, before we vote for tax cuts, we ought to be aware that tax cuts have an opportunity cost – in terms of higher borrowing, lower government spending and a potential to increase inequality. The key question is whether we are able to spend any tax cut more effectively than government spending on health care, security and education.

In 2003, the US President, George W Bush, proposed tax cuts on income, dividends and capital gains. In response, 450 economists (including 11 Nobel Laureates) signed a letter opposing these tax cuts. They argued that tax cuts would increase the deficit, fail to increase investment and increase inequality. Shortly after, 250 economists wrote a counter-letter arguing that tax cuts were fiscally responsible and would improve economic growth. It's an issue that divides the economic profession.

The case for tax cuts

Greg Mankiw (b. 1958), an economist who advised the Bush administration, made a strong case for the tax cuts on the basis that they would increase the incentives for high-income earners to work. Mankiw argues that high marginal tax rates discourage work and enterprise and lead to a deadweight welfare loss (*see* page 71) of lost output.

If you feel guilty about voting for tax cuts for yourself, you can console yourself that if tax cuts encourage entrepreneurship and greater productivity, it is not just you who benefits but the whole economy. David Stockman, who for a time was President Reagan's budget director, once argued that the benefits of tax cuts would "trickle down" (*see* page 11) to everyone in the economy. If an entrepreneur receives a tax cut, he can invest more, creating more employment, and – so the theory goes – everyone will benefit.

"[The tax cuts proposal] is fiscally responsible and it will create more employment, economic growth, and opportunities for all"
excerpt from 2003 letter to President Bush signed by 250 economists

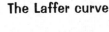

The Laffer curve

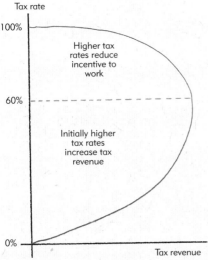

The American economist **Arthur Laffer** (b. 1940) advised the Reagan administration and also Donald Trump's 2016 presidential campaign. Laffer took the justification for tax cuts even further, arguing that cutting income tax could increase total tax revenue. He famously drew a simple diagram on the back of a napkin in a restaurant. His logic was that, if marginal income tax rates were 100%, nobody would work and the government would receive no tax. Therefore, if you cut tax to 90%, more people would work and the government would receive an increase in income tax revenue. Laffer offered a very attractive political proposition: cut income tax and gain more income tax revenue. Have your cake and eat it! Unsurprisingly, Ronald Reagan, a conservative who instinctively wanted to cut income tax, didn't take much persuading. The

Laffer curve went from the back of a napkin to a very convenient justification for the 1980s cut in US marginal rates of income tax.

Free market economists such as **Friedrich Hayek** argue that most government spending tends to be inefficient, therefore cutting taxes enables the economy to reduce wasteful and overbearing government intervention and allow individuals to keep a higher proportion of their rewards from work.

So far, we have a fairly convincing economic case for income tax cuts which, combined with a natural personal preference for lower taxes, makes a vote for tax cuts appear very attractive. However, other economists take a different view.

The case against tax cuts

Firstly, some economists doubt that cutting tax rates actually increases revenue. **Paul Krugman**, a critic of the George W Bush tax cuts, argued in 2007 it was a fantasy that tax cuts would alone increase tax revenue.

Economic theory:

An income tax cut can create incentives to work but may lead to lower tax revenue and the opportunity cost of spending cuts.

BENEFITS OF
TAX CUTS

This was for a few reasons. The Laffer curve may work at rates of 90%, but marginal income tax rates in the US and Europe are closer to 35–50%. You can't keep cutting tax rates and hoping people will respond by increasing average hours worked. Although lower taxes make work relatively more attractive than leisure because of the substitution effect, there is also an income effect (*see* page 93). If tax is cut, you can gain your target income by working fewer hours. Therefore, it is not guaranteed that everyone will respond to tax cuts by working more.

More importantly, we have to bear in mind that income tax cuts have an opportunity cost – lower spending or higher borrowing. As the free market economist **Milton Friedman** stated, government spending

levels are the real guide to true tax levels. In other words, income tax cuts may look attractive in the short term, but without spending cuts how will they be financed? If tax cuts do not correspond to lower spending, they will lead to higher borrowing and then the tax cuts may prove only temporary – in the long term, taxes may have to rise to pay back borrowing. If you vote for tax cuts, the question is whether this is sustainable in the long term.

We may want income tax cuts but do we want the spending cuts that will finance them? Are we able to use the extra money from a tax cut more efficiently than the government? If we receive a tax cut, the

COSTS OF
TAX CUTS

"Supply side doctrine, which claimed without evidence that tax cuts would pay for themselves, never got any traction in the world of professional economic research, even among conservatives"
Paul Krugman

government may have less money for road repairs. Therefore, the opportunity cost of the tax cut is more potholes in our roads and, as a consequence, we will need to spend more on vehicle repairs. Economists such as **Paul Samuelson** and **Joseph Stiglitz** remind us that the free market is very poor at providing public goods like roads, national security and police. In this case, the income tax cut is a false economy. We save money on income tax but then have to pay for services that used to be provided by the government.

Who benefits?

Another relevant question to ask yourself is whether you will actually benefit from the tax cut. Income tax tends to be a very progressive tax, with the rich paying a higher percentage of total tax. According to the Tax Policy Center, tax cuts in the period 2004–10 saw an increase in after-tax income of 6.6% for the top 1% of income-earners. By contrast, the poorest 10% saw an increase in after-tax income of just 0.5%. From the point of view of your personal interest, income tax cuts will benefit you disproportionately if you have a high income. If your income is low, you will generally receive little benefit from income tax cuts.

The Nordic approach

A final thought about income tax cuts is to compare different countries. Nordic countries have high rates of income tax (over 50%) and so they can afford generous welfare states. They have also achieved strong economic growth in the post-war period. The US, by comparison, has lower rates of tax, but the US does not have a universal health care system so, in addition to income tax, US workers and firms have to pay for health care insurance. For what it is worth, the populations of Nordic countries tend to rate themselves very highly in happiness indexes. Before you vote for an income tax cut, ask yourself which appeals most – the high-tax, generous welfare states of the Nordic countries or the lower-tax, more free market economy of countries such as the US?

Making a decision:

Laffer and Mankiw offer good reasons to vote for tax cuts – improved incentives should increase productivity and economic growth as well as meaning more money for you. However, you may agree with Krugman that tax cuts offer no "supply side miracle" but will mean reduced quality of public services like health care and transportation. There is no so such thing as a tax cut without an opportunity cost.

Should I boycott goods made in sweatshop factories?

Nicholas Kristof • Paul Krugman • Jeffrey Sachs • Simon Kuznets • Robert Pollin
Peter B Evans • George Akerlof • Jagdish Bhagwati • Benjamin Powell

There have been various campaigns to boycott clothes and goods produced in sweatshop factories in the developing world. Campaigners argue that it is wrong to buy cheap clothes produced in factories violating basic labour standards and paying very low wages. However, economists point to the fact that, although conditions are bad by Western standards, the jobs are better than the alternatives, and these factories can play an important role in the economic development of low-income countries.

The Pulitzer Prize-winning American writer **Nicholas Kristof** (b. 1959) admits he is appalled by conditions in sweatshop factories; but after living many years in East Asia, he is aware that, for a lot of people, the alternative is to work for even lower pay in more unstable jobs. Therefore, although he understands the concerns over conditions, a blunt campaign to ban sweatshop labour could see workers forced back into worse jobs, such as sifting through garbage at a dump for less than a dollar a day.

Paul Krugman makes a similar point, asking why we should be appalled at someone working in sweatshop conditions, when their alternative is worse. Krugman notes that our distaste for sweatshop labour is probably because we benefit from this labour and feel uncomfortable with the idea that our garment is made by somebody on very low pay. However, if we boycott sweatshop labour, this may make the people we wish to help even worse off and so it may become counterproductive.

Krugman is no fan of sweatshop owners. He argues that they are often "rapacious local entrepreneurs, whose only concern [is] to take advantage of the profit opportunities offered by cheap labor". But, as he points out, for destitute parents in India the alternative to child labour might not be education, but selling their children to begging syndicates, in which children can even be mutilated to become more profitable as beggars. The point is, although we do not approve of conditions in these sweatshop factories, the alternative may be very much worse.

"My concern is not that there are too many sweatshops but that there are too few"
Jeffrey Sachs

Are sweatshops necessary for economic development?

Furthermore, **Jeffrey Sachs** who was special adviser to two former UN Secretaries General, argues that sweatshop factories can be a necessary stage in economic development. If firms can offer manufacturing jobs, it takes the pressure off the land and also helps agricultural wages to rise. He also points out that many countries which are now considered developed, such as South Korea, Taiwan and Singapore, went through a stage of sweatshop manufacturing, which enabled a general rise in living standards and eventual improvement in factory conditions – like the Western world experienced at the turn of the 20th century. Sachs argues that the best way for Africa to develop from its "backbreaking rural poverty" would be to encourage sweatshop factories, which provide alternatives to the incredibly low-paid and unstable subsistence farming.

However, not all economists are convinced about the merit of supporting sweatshop conditions. The Russian–American Nobel Laureate economist and statistician **Simon Kuznets** (1901–85) argued there is no guarantee that rapid industrialization will lead to an equitable distribution of this economic development. Kuznets claimed that firms that ran sweatshops could make monopoly profits through the unfair treatment of workers. He argued that, through suitable labour codes, unions and regulations, sweatshop conditions could be improved without holding back economic development.

John Miller, an American economist who criticizes the mainstream economic view on sweatshops, argues that campaigners are right to put pressure on multinationals to improve working conditions and pay – especially when evidence of worker mistreatment includes "illegally collected

Would you pay an extra 50 cents to enable better pay and conditions for workers in sweatshops?

> *"The anti-sweatshop movement is taking constructive steps toward improving living and working conditions for millions of poor people throughout the world"*
> Robert Pollin

fines, confiscated identity papers, and beatings". Miller also cites surveys which state that consumers would be willing to pay a small premium to contribute toward better conditions for workers in sweatshops.

Should we campaign for higher wages?

A study by the American economist **Robert Pollin** (b. 1950) found that US retail prices for clothing would need to rise only by 1.8% in order to cover a 100% wage increase for sweatshop workers in Mexican garment factories. This means that, with a sweatshop premium, a casual shirt would rise from just $32 to $32.50. In this regard, consumers can have the best of both worlds – cheap clothes from developing countries, but also the knowledge that their clothes are not the result of "unfairly low" wages.

Classical economists caution that high wages are likely to cause unemployment. But this assumes a static labour market. The American political sociologist **Peter B Evans** (b. 1944) notes that higher wages can lead to increased spending in the economy and boost overall demand. This "high road" to development can lead to faster improvements in living standards than merely relying on ultra-low wages.

Another argument for pushing for higher wages is the efficiency wage theory (*see* page 96). **George Akerlof** argues that if workers are malnourished and tired from working long hours, higher wages could help increase

productivity, and therefore raising wages would not be as counterproductive as firms or economists may fear.

However, other economists caution against the view that rising wages will automatically lead to increased welfare. Firstly, as the Indian–American economist **Jagdish Bhagwati** states, if wages rise to provide our concept of a *living wage* (the amount a person needs to cover the basic cost of living), the competitive advantage of that country may be lost. If we pay a living wage for a very poor country like Ghana, it may encourage the firm to shift production to a more capital-intensive, middle-income country like Malaysia. In other words, our good intentions to raise wages for the working poor in Ghana could lead to these jobs being lost. American economist **Benjamin Powell** (b. 1978) has noted that the activist group "Shop with a Conscience Consumer Guide" listed 41 approved sweat-free factories, but 29 are in the US and Canada and only one in Asia. It doesn't help the most acute poverty levels if factories can't set up in the poorest countries.

Furthermore, raising wages above *market equilibrium* (where supply equals demand) can lead to unintended consequences. Nicholas Kristof found evidence from Cambodia that well-meaning attempts to pay sweatshop labour above market wages often led to those in charge of jobs demanding bribes of up to a month's salary in exchange for a job.

Can campaigns improve things?

There appears a strong economic case to be cautious about campaigns that lead to sweatshop factories being closed. However, before we surrender to the remorseless logic of market forces, consider a study by Denis Arnold and Laura Hartman. They documented how, under pressure from public opinion, large multinationals have voluntarily undertaken measures to improve working conditions without harming their competitive advantage. In particular, they note that footwear manufacturers Adidas-Salomon and Nike have altered their production techniques. Rather than just outsource production to the lowest-cost suppliers, these multinationals have undertaken to be responsible for the conditions of workers in a way that doesn't disrupt the jobs and salaries they depend on. After finding that their Vietnam factories relied heavily on child labour, they required the supplier to provide education and a guaranteed job at the end of it.

Furthermore, Arnold and Hartman note that these beneficial changes to working

Economic theory:

Sweatshop jobs may appear very harsh and low-paid by our standards, but they are better than the alternatives in poor countries. This is why people are willing to work there.

conditions can have innumerable benefits which help retain profitability. Workers are more productive and loyal to the company, and better working conditions can provide a unique selling point for the firm – or at least avoid the damaging PR from the exposure of harsh labour conditions. In other words, campaigns and the threat of boycotts can shift corporate attitudes so large multinationals implement better working practices in a way that does not lead to job losses or worse alternatives.

Making a decision:

It is hard to disagree with Paul Krugman that a complete boycott of goods that leads to the factory closing down is likely to make the affected workers worse off. Nevertheless, the study by Arnold and Hartman suggests that a more nuanced approach of putting pressure on multinationals to improve conditions can help improve welfare for workers in developing economies and make us feel better about the clothes we import.

Should I support government subsidies for a local firm facing bankruptcy?

Friedrich Hayek • Joseph Schumpeter • Mark Thoma • Larry Summers
Alan Krueger • Paul Krugman • Milton Friedman

When a large employer goes bankrupt, it can lead to very high costs in terms of unemployment and lower standards of living. Almost overnight, prosperous areas can become ghost towns. Faced with this prospect, it is understandable that we might want governments to subsidize and prevent the bankruptcy of these struggling firms. However, economists generally argue that subsidies merely delay the inevitable and waste taxpayers' money to prop up inefficient and declining firms.

Many economists are passionate about the idea of letting failing firms go bankrupt. **Friedrich Hayek** argued that government intervention in industry was doomed to failure because politicians respond to short-term political pressures rather than economic logic. For example, once governments start intervening, they feel obliged to prevent job losses, even if it means keeping workers in unproductive jobs. In 1920, the UK coal industry employed 1.2 million miners. Ninety years later the number had fallen to 5,000. Hayek would argue that this overwhelming and inevitable change in the economy is not something that can be held back by government subsidy. To Hayek it may be unfortunate if businesses close, but it would be more unfortunate for a government to intervene and waste money in a forlorn attempt to overcome market forces.

A similar idea was suggested by **Joseph Schumpeter**. In fact, he argued that the failure of inefficient firms is the best thing that can happen for the economy – this process of weeding out failing firms allows more efficient businesses to take their place. Schumpeter called this process creative destruction (*see* page 132). Therefore, rather than feeling bad about an old cotton firm closing down, we should be grateful that in its place better-paid jobs will eventually come. If this sounds aloof and hard-hearted, Schumpeter might ask whether you really would prefer the very low-paid jobs that were available in your town 100 years ago.

Softening the blow

However, one problem with that *laissez-faire* approach (free from government interference) to declining industries is that it can seem very heartless to someone caught up in the reality of losing their job. For those directly affected by unemployment, it is little comfort to hear an economist claim that in the long-term this factory closure will maximize economic efficiency. Economists such as **Mark Thoma**

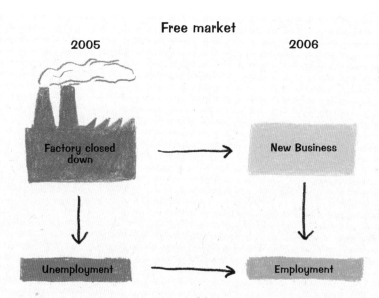

Free market

2005   **2006**

Factory closed down → New Business

Unemployment → Employment

A factory closing down causes short-run problems of unemployment but, in the long run, new business are formed creating employment.

(b. 1956) take a more nuanced approach, suggesting that government subsidies and tax-credits can help areas that are undergoing rapid structural change. Here government intervention can lessen the localized costs of industrial decline and structural unemployment. It is not easy for an unemployed former car worker to retrain and then gain a new job in an emerging industry without assistance. Government subsidies to help relocate and retrain workers can allow a more managed decline.

A majority of economists are opposed to state support for declining industries, but there are exceptions. For example, in 2008 the US car industry was in crisis, with two major car firms, GM and Chrysler, facing bankruptcy. The economic costs were predicted to be very high, not just in terms of job losses in the car industry but also in all the knock-on effects for related service industries.

Larry Summers (b. 1954), an American economist who has held senior positions in the US Treasury Department and World Bank, examined the state of the US auto industry and considered the likely outcomes of government intervention versus a laissez-faire approach. On balance, he felt there was a case for a government bailout and subsidy. Summers helped craft a bailout that allowed

"For me, the main lesson was that in a crisis, economic policy makers have to take actions that they would not ordinarily take"
Alan Krueger

a managed bankruptcy, with government subsidies of $78.2 billion. The bailout provided time for the US car industry to restructure and recover. Jobs were saved but, importantly, the industry defied expectations to return to profitability. Firms also paid back $58 billion of the original subsidies. It is a reminder that firms on the edge of bankruptcy are not necessarily "structural inefficient and doomed to decline" as Schumpeter might have argued.

While it would be a mistake always to campaign for subsidies for failing firms, it doesn't mean we should always oppose them. The American economist **Alan Krueger** (b. 1960) was initially sceptical about the desirability of a government bailout. He noted the previous failed attempts at restructuring and the plummeting sales suggesting long-term decline. However,

Subsidies

✓	✗
YES	**NO**
Temporary support in difficult times	Can't hold back changing times
Protect against unemployment	Higher taxes/prices for everyone else
Managed decline	Prevents new firms coming
	Creates pressure groups

after the apparent success of the bailout, Krueger admitted it was more successful than he expected and showed that "economists should be less doctrinaire".

While industrial firms rarely get economic support for government bailouts, banks are generally a different case. When Lehman Brothers was allowed to go bankrupt in 2008, it caused a financial and economic crisis. **Paul Krugman** argues that, in the case of banks, the government has no option but to protect institutions and people's confidence in the banking system. He argues that the big mistake of the Great Depression was to allow banks to fail and people to lose confidence in the banking system. Banks may not deserve a bailout, but we bail them out because the alternative is much worse.

Side effects of subsidies

Despite the success of some government subsidies and bailouts, other economists are unconvinced, maintaining that government subsidy sets a dangerous precedent that becomes hard to overturn. Back in the 1930s, the Great Depression led to plummeting farm prices and incomes of US farmers. Given the real hardship endured by the farmers, the federal government stepped in to prevent the worst poverty, subsidizing farmers by guaranteeing minimum prices for the first time. Even though there was social justification for such intervention, **Milton Friedman** was unconvinced, arguing that agricultural subsidies are inefficient and expensive for both the taxpayer and the consumer. Friedman noted that when subsidies were given to farmers, it created a very powerful political pressure group who become determined to hold on to subsidies.

Now, long after those first agricultural subsidies, the programme is flourishing. Friedman argued that the real problem is that the benefits of subsidies are very visible to farmers, but the costs are more diffuse and invisible to everyone else. But the fact remains – because of subsidies, we pay higher prices for food and higher taxes, and the policy discourages innovation and measures to increase efficiency. In other words, Friedman felt that before eagerly backing government subsidies, we should be more aware of the invisible costs to us and everyone else in the economy.

Another example supporting the case against government subsidies was Concorde, a luxury jet supported by the French and British governments. With supersonic speed, it could cross the Atlantic in half the time of a regular passenger jet. With its small

Economic theory:

If firms go bankrupt, free market economics suggests that the best option is to let them fail and allow new, more efficient firms to take their place.

capacity and high costs, the plane was inefficient and loss-making, but because of prior political commitments both British and French governments ended up giving ongoing subsidies to keep the flagship plane in operation. Friedman would argue that taxpayers were effectively subsidizing business passengers as they enjoyed caviar and champagne on their three-and-a-half-hour transatlantic flight – not the best use of taxpayers' money.

Making a decision:

Milton Friedman makes a convincing case that government subsidies invariably end up propping up inefficient firms, which have large costs to the taxpayer. However, you may prefer the analysis of Larry Summers, that in particular cases a subsidy can help overcome short-term issues and more effectively manage decline so the local job losses are less painful.

Will I be better off with tariffs on imports?

David Ricardo • Friedrich List • Joan Robinson • Ha-Joon Chang
John Maynard Keynes • Greg Mankiw • Milton Friedman • Joseph Stiglitz

If there is one thing economists are supposed to agree on, it is the idea that free trade is good, and protectionism is bad. There is general agreement that tariffs on imports will make you worse off. Yet, despite this economic consensus, free trade still gets a bad press, and many politicians argue that higher tariffs are a way to protect domestic industries, diversify the economy and raise living standards. There are also economists who will stand above the parapet and argue that some tariffs may actually be justified.

In the 19th century, **David Ricardo** developed a *theory of comparative advantage* – the idea that countries should specialize in what they are comparatively best at. Ricardo used the example that if Great Britain is relatively inefficient in producing wine, it should import wine from a country like Portugal. To Ricardo, it would make no sense to put tariffs on imports of wine, just to protect a few English wine producers.

According to a theory that Ricardo developed, known as the *Ricardian trade theory*, the only groups who benefit from tariffs are owners and workers from internationally uncompetitive businesses.

In favour of tariffs...sometimes

An argument in favour of tariffs was made by the German economist **Friedrich List** (1789–1845). List argued that tariffs were important for enabling new industries to develop. This argument has become known as the *infant industry argument*. List argued

that free trade benefits established economies and industries that are already developed. However, if a primarily agricultural economy wants to diversify into manufacturing, it needs a period of tariff protection so the industry can grow, develop economies of scale and become efficient. Insisting on universal free trade would hold back less developed economies.

The 20th-century British economist **Joan Robinson** also criticized Ricardo's theory of comparative advantage. She argued that, although Ricardo was correct to say that free trade benefited Great Britain, in Portugal the potential benefits were not so clear. The Portuguese economy was less developed, and free trade caused it to become stuck producing low-income agricultural products.

This infant industry argument has received increased attention in recent years. Critics of globalization argue that unfair applications of free trade explain part of the gap between the developing and developed world. In *Kicking Away the Ladder* (2002), the South Korean economist **Ha-Joon Chang** offers many examples of developed countries going through a period of protectionism while they develop new industries. Once they are established and dominant, these developed countries then have a vested interest in promoting free trade and insisting that everyone else removes tariffs, too.

List, Robinson and Chang advise that if you live in the developed world, you have a vested interest in free trade and will probably benefit from lower tariffs. However, if you live in an underdeveloped economy, primarily based on agriculture, the story is different – tariffs may enable you to get better-paid jobs in new, higher-value industries.

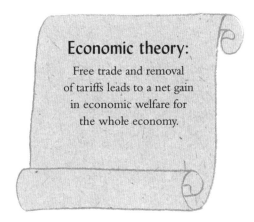

Economic theory:
Free trade and removal of tariffs leads to a net gain in economic welfare for the whole economy.

New industries need protection in order to grow and flourish.

More than money

However, some argue that it's not just about the money. Tariffs and protectionism create national rivalry, while free trade is a signal of international cooperation. Writing in the aftermath of World War I, **John Maynard Keynes** felt that free trade could help promote international cooperation and reduce national rivalries.

Keynes said that there is nothing intrinsically better about coal dug up in your own country of Brazil than coal imported from across the border in Argentina. But because protectionism and the desire to limit this free movement of goods create an insular attitude and lower living standards, the removal of tariffs represents faith in a more internationalist outlook.

Free trade: the good and the bad

There are plenty of other free market economists, such as **Greg Mankiw** and **Milton Friedman**, who would agree that if you want an improvement in living

> *"Yet economics teaches that international trade is not like war but can be win-win"*
> Greg Mankiw

standards, vote for free trade and the removal of tariffs. They argue that Ricardo's theory of comparative advantage states that removing tariffs improves living standards – even if other countries don't reciprocate. Therefore, free trade can be beneficial – even if unilateral. Friedman was critical of the political obsession with increasing exports. He argued that our living standards are highest when we maximize imports and minimize exports, and this can be encouraged by reducing import tariffs.

But if Friedman is correct, why are so many people suspicious, if not actually fearful, of free trade? **Joseph Stiglitz** is critical of an unwavering faith in free trade. He argues that although free trade has the potential to raise living standards, there is no guarantee that it will. For example, classical models are too simplistic, assuming that workers who are unemployed (because of the effects of free trade) can easily find new jobs, which is often not the case.

Economics theory suggests that, mathematically, an economy will have a *net gain* from free trade – the benefits will be higher than the cost. But, Stiglitz asks, is there any guarantee that the losers will be compensated? He argues that rising inequality in recent decades suggests this is not the case. If we work in certain industries, tariffs may help protect our jobs in the short term.

Free trade is a cornerstone of economic faith, with good reason. Generally, a reduction in tariffs will improve living standards, especially for consumers. However, this does not mean that every move toward free trade is necessarily advantageous. There may be cases where tariffs play a role in creating a more diverse economy and help economic development.

Making a decision:

If you are a consumer in a developed economy, you will see a clear benefit from pursuing the free trade approach of David Ricardo. However, if you live in a developing economy and are in a low-paid agricultural job, you might see a strong case for tariffs, to enable new infant industries to develop to give the economy a chance for diversification.

Should I welcome parking charges in my street and city?

Adam Smith • Arthur Pigou • Donald Shoup • Tyler Cowen • Mark Thoma

We can happily pay $3 for a cup of coffee, but the idea of paying $3 for parking while we drink the coffee creates much more antagonism. We often exhibit strong preferences for free parking as a kind of natural right. However, economists who focus on opportunity cost argue that, just as there is no such thing as a free lunch, there is also no such thing as free parking. As a result, some economists are keen to make payment for parking more universal and more expensive. But will we be convinced by these arguments of efficiency and opportunity cost?

When **Adam Smith** wrote his 1776 book *The Wealth of Nations*, he was concerned with the market mechanism and how firms and consumers respond to market prices. The problem with this free market approach is that it ignores the costs and benefits that impact other people not involved in the transaction. In 1920, **Arthur Pigou** investigated the existence of these external costs (*see* page 13) of economic actions and found examples where the social cost of a decision was higher than the private cost. Pigou used an example of firms constructing a factory in a busy residential area, causing pollution and congestion to those who live nearby. This *theory of externalities* can equally be applied to the modern problem of traffic congestion.

Cost of free car parking spaces

The American economist and urban planner **Donald Shoup** (b. 1938) has spent many years investigating the cost of free parking, arguing that it has distorted the design of cities, has created more pollution and more congestion and, in 2002, gave an inefficient subsidy worth $127 billion to cars.

Shoup argues that if there is a critical mass of people wanting to park for free, then demand becomes greater than supply, which creates several external costs for other inhabitants of the city – one of which is the need to spend more time driving around the city looking for a free parking space. A lack of parking spaces adds to the gridlock and congestion, which wastes our time. In addition, if we spend more time driving around trying to find a space, we create more pollution, which leads to worse air quality and poorer health.

Because people expect to park for free (99% of journeys in the US end in a free parking space), cities have given over substantial space for parking. Given the price of city centres and the shortage of housing, these scarce plots of land are actually very expensive.

Shoup claims that in 2012 the cost of building a parking spot in an average American

"Every tax, however, is to the person who pays it a badge, not of slavery but of liberty"

Adam Smith

Higher real estate prices

Free parking

city was $24,000. Also, if we use more space for parking lots, it means less space for housing and business, pushing up the cost of renting. When we get free parking, we pay for it in higher living costs, higher business rents and higher prices. If we had to pay reasonable charges for parking, we could use more land for building houses, rather than the deadweight welfare loss (*see* page 71) of parking.

Arthur Pigou claims that, to overcome market failure, the government should place a tax or charge on goods, so that we pay the full social cost. In terms of parking, the social cost estimated by Shoup is quite significant, meaning that the *socially efficient* price (the price that reflects all social costs and social benefits) of parking is much higher than we have become accustomed to. But if money raised from parking charges was invested in public transportation, it might be more attractive to residents, as they could see how it provides alternatives to inner city parking.

Side effects of parking charges

Although there is a strong economic case for parking charges, other economists warn that there may be unintended consequences of charging for parking. The American

economist **Tyler Cowen** warns that, if you start charging for parking, it has to be applied everywhere, otherwise it merely shifts the problem from one part of town to another. For example, if you introduce parking charges in the city centre, shoppers may just drive even farther, to out-of-town shopping malls, creating more traffic and congestion on the outskirts while leaving city centres like ghost towns. Another unintended consequence could be that if parking is expensive in city centres, people switch to shopping online, and soon the city is full of delivery trucks making internet deliveries.

Another reason we may oppose car parking charges is the issue of *equity* (fairness). Responding to the issue of government-controlled parking spaces, the American economist **Mark Thoma** raises the question of whether pricing issues will be fair. He argues that we need to make sure parking charges don't exclude certain segments of the population from access to certain places. For example, if parking by museums or

> **Economic theory:**
> The price of parking should reflect the full social cost – including all externalities, such as congestion, pollution and wasted space.

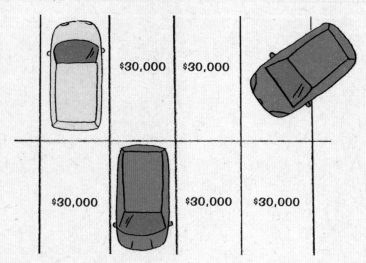

In some inner cities, the value of land for car-parking space is valued at $30,000.

national parks were very expensive, it might discourage low-income groups from visiting and so make certain places more elitist. However, as we have seen, Donald Shoup asserts that free parking hurts the poor by increasing scarcity of land and pushing up rents. Also, the very poorest may not even have a car and would benefit from increased investment in public transport instead.

If you remain unconvinced by all this economic theory, and would still like to resist parking charges, there is another issue – one of practicality. The American urban-planning academic Michael Manville admits that implementing new parking charges can be much harder in practice than in theory, for example because of the problem of people parking and avoiding the charge they are supposed to pay. Manville also notes the highly political problem of possible exploitation of disabled placard signs to avoid parking charges. Even the best economic ideas and theories don't necessarily translate into practical policy on the ground.

Making a decision:

If we hate driving around the block looking for a space, the policies of Donald Shoup suggest we would be much better off asking our council to impose parking meters. However, we may worry, like Tyler Cowen, that a city-wide parking charge could, in the long term, cause people to take their business elsewhere.

Should I support the legalization of drugs?

Milton Friedman • Mark Thornton • Robert Barro • Jeffrey Miron
Gary Becker • Mark H Moore • Irving Fisher

Illegal drugs can damage both individual lives and the communities where drug addicts live. Yet many economists argue that efforts at prohibition not only have failed to halt drug use but also have created a powerful criminal black market – which is more damaging and dangerous than the drugs themselves. However, critics of legalization fear that decriminalization could see a further rise in drug use, which would be harmful for both users and wider society.

Problems of prohibition

Milton Friedman argued that the prohibition of drugs and attempts to limit supply merely create a thriving black market which benefits the criminal gangs who supply the drugs. Furthermore, to feed their habit and pay black market prices, drug users often resort to crime. According to Friedman, prohibition of drugs is responsible for higher homicide rates, burglary and general lawlessness. According to the US Department of Justice, half of federal inmates reported drug use in the month before their offence.

Friedman argued that although a "war on drugs" may be politically appealing, in practice governments are fighting a losing battle, wasting billions of dollars in a vain attempt to limit supply. The policy of prohibition is also responsible for an explosion in prison populations, leading to increased government spending and young lives wasted. Friedman notes that, even if governments are successful in seizing quantities of drugs, it merely raises the market price, creating a greater incentive for people with poor prospects to be drawn into the criminal world of drug supply.

According to **Mark Thornton** (b. 1960), an American economist and a leading expert on drug prohibition, its failure has a clear parallel in the link between alcohol prohibition and organized crime in the period 1920–33. Before 1920, the homicide rate in the US was 6 per 100,000 people, but within 13 years, this had risen to nearly 10 per 100,000. The repeal of Prohibition in 1933 reversed

Costs of drug prohibition

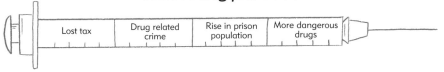

| Lost tax | Drug related crime | Rise in prison population | More dangerous drugs |

Costs of drug legalization

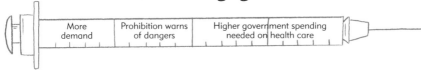

More demand | Prohibition warns of dangers | Higher government spending needed on health care

this trend in violent crime, and 10 years later the homicide rate had halved. Supporters of drug legalization argue that the renewed surge in violent crime rates of the 1970s and 1980s was at least partly due to the then-President Richard Nixon's high-profile war on drugs in 1971.

Robert Barro (b. 1944) argues that the distortionary effect of drugs prohibition is not limited to crime, but has even extended to foreign policy and trade deals. In particular, US efforts to root out supply have led to deterioration in relations with foreign countries that grow the raw drugs.

While America suffers from drug-related violence, economist Daniel Mejía argues that countries such as Colombia and Mexico, on the front line of illegal drug production, have witnessed far higher social costs, with shocking rates of violence, homicide and corruption. In Colombia, the homicide rate peaked at 70 per 100,000 people in 1999 during the war on the Medellín drug cartel.

Another unwanted side effect of drug prohibition is to increase the potency (and potential danger) of drugs. Mark Thornton refers to the "Iron law of prohibition" – "the harder the enforcement, the harder the drugs". During alcohol prohibition, spirits became cheaper than more bulky beer, causing a rise in demand for spirits. Thornton makes a similar argument that prohibition of drugs has led to the rise of more potent and

dangerous forms such as crack cocaine and crystal meth. Legalization would, at least, help avoid the most dangerous, and potentially toxic, forms of drugs.

Another powerful argument for drug legalization is made by the American economist **Jeffrey Miron** (b. 1957), who specializes in the economics of illegal drugs. He argues that drug legalization would redistribute income from criminal gangs to the public purse. Miron puts an estimate of $41.3 billion on the cost of the US trying to enforce laws related to drug prohibition. He argues that, rather than trying to stop supply (which has never succeeded), federal funds would be better targeted at trying to reduce demand, through education and drug treatment programmes.

Tax revenue from legal drugs

Most economists who support the legalization of drugs argue that it should be combined with a "sin tax" to make the price relatively high and increase tax revenues. Robert Barro argues for drug legalization using a similar structure as for cigarettes – this involves substantial tax rates, restrictions on sales to minors and campaigns to raise awareness of health costs. The advantage of using cigarette-style tax rates is that it would overcome the issue of drug pushers giving away cheap drugs until people are addicted and then charging extortionate prices, which force addicts into crime to feed their habit. **Gary Becker** – one of the first economists to specialize in drug addiction and other sociological issues – concurred, arguing that the money raised from drug taxes could be used to help deal with problems of addiction and to educate youngsters about the dangers of drugs.

Would legalization increase demand?

If there is such strong support for drug legalization from economists, why do many of us recoil from the idea of making drugs legal? The main concern is that legalization would lead to an increase in the use of these dangerous drugs. As Milton Friedman himself admitted, if you legalize drugs and destroy the black market, the price of drugs would fall "and as an economist, lower prices tend to generate more demand". Furthermore, there is a precedent for legalization leading to a rapid increase in drug use. In the decade following the end of Prohibition in the US in 1933, alcohol consumption in the country shot up. The American economist **Paul Taubman** argued that legalization and lower prices would increase demand and create more drug addicts. This would be a very high cost to both individual drug users and communities, where drug use can damage mental faculties.

Also, some economists argue that the lessons of alcohol prohibition are not applicable to more damaging drugs such as heroin and cocaine. Society's use of alcohol has long been widespread, so it was to be expected that people would try to continue their old habits during Prohibition. But **Mark H Moore** (b. 1947), author of books including *Recognizing Public Value* (2013), argues that the real lesson of Prohibition is that society can make a dent in the consumption of drugs. He points to heroin and cocaine as examples of dangerous drugs that are mostly unpopular. Despite the challenges of enforcing drug prohibition, legalization could slowly change attitudes and increase their use over time.

Miron argues that if drug prohibition fails to reduce consumption, it is unambiguously inferior to legalization. But if legalization does increase use, this presents a severe challenge to the case for legalization. While some economists will make the case to legalize all drugs, recent efforts have often focused on softer drugs, such as cannabis,

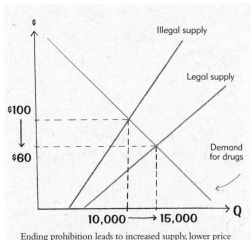

Ending prohibition leads to increased supply, lower price and greater quantity (Q) demanded.

171

which is believed to have less toxic effects. Some countries and American states have voted to legalize marijuana. However, the evidence is mixed. One study, by Robert J MacCoun, of the Dutch experience of legalizing marijuana sales, found that between 1997 and 2005 cannabis use by Dutch 15–24-year-olds dropped from 14.3% to 11.4%. There was also evidence that legal sales had reduced contact between marijuana users and hard-drug sellers. Less welcome were the estimated one million annual "cannabis tourists" who visited Amsterdam marijuana shops to take advantage of the drug's legal status.

Many economists approach this topic from a utilitarian perspective, but some are more concerned about the moral implications of drug use. The American economist and social campaigner **Irving Fisher** was a strong advocate of alcohol prohibition, arguing that prohibition could save us from ourselves.

Economic theory:

Drug prohibition imposes severe costs related to the criminal activity surrounding illegal supply. Prohibition would save money, make drugs less dangerous and reduce criminal activity.

Fisher was concerned about alcohol but this paternalistic view could easily apply to marijuana; reports have suggested it can lead to long-term problems of mental health, anxiety, memory loss, even psychosis. To Fisher, drugs are demerit goods (*see* page 53) – something the government should legislate against to prevent people making the wrong decisions.

Making a decision:

You may agree with Friedman that legalization of drugs will do much to reduce crime rates and the cost of trying to implement unenforceable laws. However, if you agree with Taubman that legalization will increase demand, you may feel it is a price not worth paying as we need to make a strong statement about the moral and personal damage from taking drugs.

Should I worry about my government getting into debt?

Adam Smith • John Maynard Keynes • Carmen Reinhart • Kenneth Rogoff
Paul Krugman • L Randall Wray

When we hear about record levels of government debt, the figures can seem overwhelming, raising the prospect of unsustainable debt and a burden for future generations. Yet economists are often much more sanguine about government debt. In fact, Keynes created a whole new branch of economics that justified government borrowing – exactly at the time that conventional wisdom suggested doing the opposite.

A "pernicious system"?

Classical economists typically took a dim view of government borrowing. **Adam Smith** argued that this "pernicious system of funding" impaired the capacity of entrepreneurs to invest and severely retarded the "natural progress of a nation towards wealth and prosperity". He warned that high levels of government borrowing could lead to default, devaluation of currency, inflation and capital flight. Smith was making an argument known as *crowding out*. This is the observation that governments borrow by selling bonds to the private sector (such as individuals, banks and pension funds): if the private sector buys bonds, it has less capital to fund more efficient private sector spending and investment.

Despite the classical economists' dim view of debt, public sector debt in the UK in the period of Smith and Ricardo was higher than in modern times. In 1822, UK debt reached the level of 185% of GDP, but despite this seemingly high level of debt, it wasn't the constraint to UK economic growth that Smith and Ricardo feared. Nevertheless, up until the 1930s, a balanced budget remained a cornerstone of classical economics, perhaps helped by intuitive ideas of "sound finances" and "balancing the household budget". So, if a balanced budget makes good sense, why did **John Maynard Keynes** seem to throw the old orthodoxies out of the window?

"Nature's remedy" in a recession

The Great Depression of the 1930s changed everything: the decade saw a global collapse in output, a rise in unemployment and a deep recession. Understandably, private individuals responded to this economic catastrophe by saving more, but this only served to cause a further fall in demand, something Keynes called the paradox of thrift (*see* page 135). Keynes argued that, given this slump in demand, the government should intervene and make use of all the surplus, unused savings and idle resources (such as unemployed people) – in other words, the government should borrow! In the context of recession, government spending would not crowd out the private sector, but kickstart the economy.

At the time, Keynes's radical policy suggestions were challenged by classical

173

"To 'dig holes in the ground', paid for out of savings, will increase, not only employment, but the real national dividend of useful goods and services"

John Maynard Keynes

economists, who retorted that we couldn't afford to borrow and, in the long term, markets would clear. But Keynes was dismissive of the idea that in the long run everything would be fine, and famously remarked, "In the long-run we are all dead". He saw the damage of unemployment and wanted the government to act now. To him, it was irresponsible to do nothing and accept mass unemployment as something out of your control. In this situation, Keynes saw government borrowing not as something just to be tolerated, but as something to be welcomed – because government borrowing and *deficit spending* (higher government spending financed by borrowing rather than by raising tax) could ease the pain of the recession and end the wastage of resources.

The important thing is that Keynes advocated higher borrowing in a recession – contrary to popular belief, he wasn't in favour of higher borrowing per se. If

> # Economic theory:
> Keynesian theory suggests that, in a recession, borrowing is desirable. However, during a period of normal growth, debt has economic costs.

borrowing in a recession is good, then during a boom the government should run a balanced budget or even a surplus to reduce net debt. In other words, in a recession borrowing is fine – desirable even – but in periods of normal economic growth it is a different matter.

Despite the work of John Maynard Keynes, persistent fears over government debt have remained – from both politicians and economists. After the 2008 financial crisis, there was renewed concern over the exponential growth in government debt levels, especially in such countries as Greece, Spain and Ireland.

Fears about budget deficits

In 2010, the economists **Carmen Reinhart** and **Kenneth Rogoff** produced a paper "Growth in a Time of Debt" that argued that government borrowing of over 90% of GDP was associated with lower rates of economic growth. These findings were controversial, but seemed to suggest we should worry

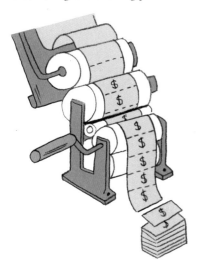

> *"So what does government borrowing do? It gives some of those excess savings a place to go — and in the process expands overall demand, and hence GDP. It does NOT crowd out private spending"*
> Paul Krugman

about rising government debt. They were picked up by politicians and bankers keen to promote austerity. In particular, Jean-Claude Trichet, then president of the European Central Bank, pushed European countries to cut their deficits. He argued that spending cuts and deficit reduction would boost confidence and help recovery.

Despite the political appeal of austerity, post-2008 there was also a resurgence of interest in the work of Keynes. **Paul Krugman** was a leading advocate of Keynesian deficit spending. Claiming that fears over budget deficits were largely political and were bad economics, he argued that austerity in Europe was damaging to the

European economies and proof that austerity could be self-defeating, causing GDP to shrink. Krugman said that in this era of low interest rates, governments could and should borrow more.

The economist **L Randall Wray** (b. 1953) is a proponent of *Modern Monetary Theory (MMT)*, which suggests that the problem of government debt is greatly exaggerated. But the exception is countries who issue *non-sovereign debt* — i.e., not in their own currency. As Wray explains, this was an issue for countries in the eurozone such as Greece, Portugal and Ireland. Without their own currency and Central Bank they were vulnerable to *capital flight* (mass exodus from the country of financial assets and capital) leading to higher bond yields. However, a country (such as the UK or the US) with its own currency has the ability to provide liquidity and buy bonds if necessary.

LOAN APPROVED

Making a decision:
In normal circumstances, you may agree that high debt levels can cause the problems that Smith and Ricardo forecast. However, in recession you may prefer the Keynesian solution to run a budget deficit to stimulate demand and reduce unemployment.

Should we worry about rising inequality?

Milton Friedman • Ludwig von Mises • Thomas Piketty • Joseph Stiglitz
Thomas Sowell • John Maynard Keynes • Paul Krugman • William Baumol
Arthur Pigou • Amartya Sen

A marked feature of the past few decades is a sharp rise in inequality in most Western economies and especially the US. With some exceptions, incomes of the top 1% have increased significantly, while median real incomes have remained relatively stagnant. Does it matter if we become better off relative to others in society? Should we pursue redistribution of wealth or celebrate the freedom to benefit from our inherently different abilities?

Benefits of inequality

Classical economists, from Adam Smith to **Milton Friedman**, have always placed great importance on the role of incentives to encourage innovation and business activity. To that end, Friedman makes three important points. First, he argues that inequality is a necessary feature of an economy; without incentives and the opportunity to earn more, the economy would become stagnant and the overall net welfare lower. Second, he says that economic inequality is an inevitable feature of a society which allows political freedom, and that a society which aims at equality will inevitably cause constraints on individual freedoms. Third, Friedman argues that inequality is actually less prevalent than it appears to be. For example, if we look at actual consumption rather than income levels, there is greater equality – many of the poorest workers in the US have relatively high levels of consumption, while the rich save.

Ludwig von Mises made a similar point supporting the desirability of inequality. Von Mises stated that at one time inequality meant low-income earners couldn't afford foreign holidays, but that as a result of economic growth everyone gets better off in absolute terms. Now even the poorest in Western society are able to afford foreign travel, plus a wide range of household appliances such as televisions. In other words, the important thing is not relative inequality but absolute income levels – as long as net welfare increases, everyone becomes better off.

Costs of inequality

The French economist **Thomas Piketty** (b. 1971), author of *Capital in the Twenty-First Century* (2013), has studied income and wealth inequality over the past 250 years. He argues that, without appropriate government intervention, income and wealth inequality continue to increase.

177

Is inequality desirable?

- Encourages investment
- Incentives to work
- Reward for work

- Diminishing utility of money
- Social division
- Inequality breeds more inequality

GOOD

BAD

His thesis is that, in a free market, the rate of return on capital (r) is greater than the rate of economic growth (g). For example, asset owners can gain interest of, say, 5%, which is higher than growth of, say, 2%. Therefore, landlords and shareholders are able to reinvest their dividends and interest in further wealth accumulation, while those on low incomes, paying high rents, are unable to accumulate any wealth at all. To Piketty, wealth inequality is a problem because it will continue to snowball.

Joseph Stiglitz argues that much of the growth in income of the wealthiest 1% in the US comes from the profit and often "undeserved bonuses" of the financial sector. He says that this sector is no longer focused on allocating capital to productive uses, but now seeks wasteful and exploitative rental opportunities, and that this is the kind of inequality we should be concerned about.

Stiglitz claims that inequality caused by competitive market pressures is desirable. However, powerful corporations and vested interests have used their influence to gain preferential political treatment. He gives examples of railroad monopolies being granted public land, privatization of public services and drugs legally sold above market price to the government. In other words, we should be concerned about inequality because economic inequality is tied up with

political inequality and profitable firms cementing their advantage in society.

Policies to reduce inequality

The American economist **Thomas Sowell** (b. 1930) argues that it is not just powerful companies who successfully lobby Congress for breaks. He claims that there is strong popular support for welfare programs: transfer payments to those on low incomes. While these programmes may be designed with the best intentions – to reduce inequality – they actually create a disincentive to work because earning more leads to a loss of welfare payments. Sowell states that this is an example of how "misplaced" policies to reduce inequality actually harm the prospects of the poor by discouraging incentives to work and encouraging a state of welfare dependency.

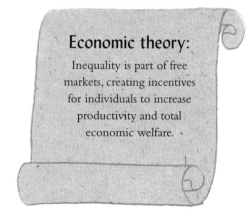

Economic theory:
Inequality is part of free markets, creating incentives for individuals to increase productivity and total economic welfare.

> *"The notion that substantial inequality is a stimulus to growth is extremely questionable"*
> William Baumol

However, **Paul Krugman** argues that the "whole poverty trap line is a falsehood wrapped in a fallacy". He claims that US welfare benefits like Medicaid and food stamps have little disincentive effect. He points to societies with high degrees of progressive tax and equality, such as Sweden, which also have high rates of innovation and business start-ups. Krugman suggests that a strong safety net and universal health care can encourage risk-taking behaviour and increase social mobility between generations – just as high inequality reduces social mobility.

The American economist **William Baumol** also argued that inequality can damage growth because high levels of poverty reduce labour productivity.

The British economist **Arthur Pigou** was concerned about inequality from the perspective of economic welfare. In the first place, he notes the diminishing returns (*see* page 51) to wealth and income. A wealthy person who gains an increase in wealth struggles actually to increase consumption because they already have enough income to buy what they need. Redistributing income to low-income groups will increase economic welfare because there is a higher marginal utility (*see* page 19) of money among those with low incomes. Second, inequality creates a sense of dissatisfaction as people feel they are falling behind their neighbours.

While inequality in the West may cause minor problems, the Indian economist **Amartya Sen** (b. 1933) argues that in the developing world inequality can be the cause of major famine. In all four devastating famines he examined, Sen found that the problem was not lack of food, but the simple fact that the poor couldn't afford to buy it, and the food was not adequately shared, creating a powerful argument to reduce global inequalities among the very poorest.

Making a decision:

If you are an entrepreneur wishing to set up a new business, you may be motivated by the thinking of Milton Friedman, who argues that incentives are necessary for encouraging growth and a rise in everyone's living standards. However, you may agree with Stiglitz and Piketty that inequality driven by inheritance and unequal political power is damaging a sense of social cohesion and fairness and is preventing a meritocracy based on fair opportunities.

Should health care be private or public?

Paul Krugman • Daniel Kahneman • Michael Rothschild • Joseph Stiglitz
• Milton Friedman • Michael D Tanner • Friedrich Hayek

The logic of markets suggests private firms are able to offer goods and services more efficiently than the public sector. Furthermore, markets enable consumers to choose between different options and create an incentive for providers to offer better quality care. However, to what extent do these arguments apply to health care? Do doctors really need a profit incentive to offer better-quality care, and to what extent are patients in a position to choose the best medical provision?

Paul Krugman argues that the best option for healthcare is universal provision by the government. If we leave it to the market, private firms will not provide healthcare unless patients pay for it. Inequality in material goods is one thing, but unequal access to healthcare questions our sense of fairness. Also, good healthcare is an important aspect of human capital – guaranteeing it to the whole population can improve the nation's health and economic efficiency.

Furthermore, private healthcare can dissuade people from seeking treatment or preventative check-ups in a timely fashion, which may be counterproductive. Krugman and Robin Wells cite a report by the Rand Corporation that found that, when people cut back on medical expenditure, they cut out not only questionable practices, but also useful medical practices. Private healthcare can encourage us to delay spending until after the optimum time. As behavioural economist **Daniel Kahneman** notes, we can't rely on consumers to be rational about long-term healthcare plans – we may lack information, place too much value on the present moment and suffer from *mental myopia* (short-sighted thinking).

Krugman argues that the American system, which relies on private health insurance, has patchy coverage, with millions of Americans going uninsured. This leads to a two-tier system, with medical bills for the uninsured becoming a major cause of bankruptcy. According to one study, three out of five bankruptcies in the US are related to unexpected medical bills. And it is not just in the US – around the world, 150 million

> *"Left to its own devices, a market economy won't care for the sick unless they can pay for it"*
> Paul Krugman

people face financial catastrophe because of their healthcare expenses. One third of these are in India, where the private sector accounts for 80% of healthcare.

Adverse selection

Another issue with private health insurance is that it can lead to the problem of adverse selection (*see* page 55). The American economists **Michael Rothschild** (b. 1942) and **Joseph Stiglitz** investigated insurance markets and found there was market failure owing to different types of insurance risk. In health insurance, young healthy individuals have a tendency not to buy insurance. Older people or those with pre-existing conditions will have a much greater incentive to take out the maximum insurance. But if healthy people don't take out insurance, health companies have a larger proportion of individuals at risk, which raises health premiums and puts off all but the most wealthy. It means those who need healthcare most often can't afford it. To overcome adverse selection in the free market requires government mandates to encourage compulsory insurance or prevent health companies refusing insurance to people with pre-existing medical conditions.

Benefits of the free market

According to **Milton Friedman**, the problem with the US healthcare system is that there is too much government intervention. He argues that the mixed system of government subsidies and private insurance offers the worst of both worlds. Because healthcare is paid for by a third party – government or private insurance companies – there has been no effort to control costs. There is a perverse incentive to spend as much as possible on healthcare because someone else is paying. Friedman explains that this is why the US spends more on healthcare – 17% of GDP – than anywhere in the world. By comparison, Canada (which has universal healthcare) spends 11% of GDP.

Friedman argues that the ideal solution would be for people to use private medical savings accounts and pay for most treatments out of this. He claims that if individuals pay for healthcare directly, they will be more careful to get lower-cost treatment and perhaps even look after their health more carefully. As Friedman notes, we are always most careful when spending our own money. He believes that insurance should only be relied on for major medical catastrophes.

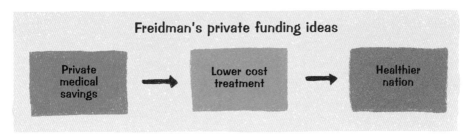

Freidman's private funding ideas

Private medical savings → Lower cost treatment → Healthier nation

Michael D Tanner (b. 1956), who heads researches into healthcare reform at the US think-tank the Cato Institute, makes a similar point. He claims that a better deal on healthcare will come from increasing competition and breaking up the cosy cartels of state health insurance companies. Allowing individuals to have portable insurance policies and be able to buy from companies in different states will force insurance companies to lower prices and create a better deal for individuals seeking insurance.

In the developing world, 80% of healthcare is supplied by private providers because government healthcare is usually underfunded. Shanta Devarajan, an economist at the World Bank, cites a study showing that private doctors were better at diagnoses, spent more time with patients and offered a better service than those in the public sector. He argues that this undermines the claim that healthcare should be provided by the government, and he suggests that the incentive of profit can lead to better-quality treatment.

"For" universal healthcare

Others argues that the nature of healthcare makes it unsuitable to the usual profit-driven dynamics of the free market. Support for universal healthcare may come from an unexpected source; in *The Road to Serfdom*

> **Economic theory:**
> Free markets are generally the most efficient way of distributing scarce resources. However, these free market principles may not apply to a public service like healthcare.

(1944), **Friedrich Hayek** made a passionate case for limiting the role of government in the economy but made an exception for the government providing basic healthcare.

While Hayek did not go into the specifics on government provision, he made the important point that in universal healthcare there is unlikely to be any moral hazard (*see* page 68). He argued that, if the government provides healthcare assistance for sickness and accident, this will not make people change their behaviour. For example, as a libertarian (*see* page 12), Hayek claimed that generous unemployment benefits could encourage people not to work. But, in the case of healthcare, government provision wouldn't encourage people to become ill.

> *"There can be no doubt that some minimum of food, shelter, and clothing, sufficient to preserve health and the capacity to work, can be assured to everybody"*
> Friedrich Hayek

Private health	Public health
Profit incentive to lower costs	Do medical staff need profit incentives?
All treatments available to those who can pay	Government limits expensive treatment of little value
Choice	How do you choose best doctor?
Lower taxes but higher insurance	Goverment can enable equity of treatment

While arguing strongly against government intervention in industry, he concludes, "The case for the state's helping to organize a comprehensive system of social insurance is very strong".

Even Milton Friedman admitted that those with single-payer, socialized healthcare, such as in Canada or Britain, were in a position to avoid excessive costs. With single-payer systems, the government acts as a monopsony buyer (*see* page 109), to pay lower prices for drugs. Healthcare can also be rationed to avoid excess use of very expensive treatments with limited benefits. Kenneth E Thorpe, a professor of health policy who coordinated ex-President Clinton's healthcare reforms, has suggested that a universal healthcare plan would save $1.1 trillion over ten years while providing comprehensive benefits to all Americans.

Paul Krugman argues that the free market ideal of a competitive healthcare market is wishful thinking. When people are ill, they don't have the time, knowledge or awareness to choose the "best" doctor. When someone is sick, the last thing you need is to have to try to choose the most cost-effective hospital. In other words, the market for healthcare is very different from markets like those for buying a car or clothes.

Making a decision:

Milton Friedman argued that competitive free markets are the most effective way for providing services, even healthcare. However, Paul Krugman points out that relying on private healthcare can lead to insufficient treatment for those on low incomes; furthermore, this under-provision of healthcare can negatively impact the wider economy.

Bibliography

Below you will find a list of sources for all quotes and diagrams featured in this book. For a fully comprehensive bibliography visit: www.economicshelp.org/keynes-biblio/

CHAPTER 1
Is it OK to be selfish?
Marx, K (1867) *The Communist Manifesto*, Preface to the first German edition. Accessed online 16 July 2017: https://www.marxists.org/archive/marx/works/1867-c1/p1.htm

Mises, L von (1985) *Theory and History*, p. 54. Auburn, AL: Mises Institute

Roosevelt, F D (1937) "Second Inaugural Address". Accessed online 16 July 2017: http://avalon.law.yale.edu/20th_century/froos2.asp

Should I park in an illegal parking space and risk a fine?
Becker, G S (1993) "The economic way of looking at behavior" (Nobel lecture), *Journal of Political Economy*, vol. 101, no. 3, pp. 385–409

What is the secret of happiness?
Scitovsky, T (1976) *Joyless Economy*, p. 103. Oxford: Oxford University Press

How can I resolve disputes with neighbours?
Coase, R (1991) "Ronald H. Coase – Prize Lecture", Nobel Media AB. Accessed online 16 July 2017: http://www.nobelprize.org/nobel_prizes/economic-sciences/laureates/1991/coase-lecture.html

Thaler, R H (2015) *Misbehaving: The Making of Behavioral Economics*, p. 142. New York: W W Norton & Co.

Is it better to gamble on the lottery or gamble by having no insurance?
Kahneman, D and Tversky, A (1979) "Prospect theory: An analysis of decision under risk", *Econometrica*, vol. 47, no. 2, pp. 263–291

Thaler, R H (2015) *Misbehaving: The Making of Behavioral Economics*, p. 18. New York: W W Norton & Co

Should I make an effort to turn off all the electric lights?
Becker, G S (1976) *The Economic Approach to Human Behavior*, p. 14. Chicago, IL: University of Chicago Press

Levin, J and Milgrom, P (2004) "Introduction to choice theory", p. 3. Stanford University

Should I bother to recycle?
Landsburg, S E (2012) *The Armchair Economist: Economics and Everyday Life*, 2nd edition, p. 284. London: Simon & Schuster

How can I lose weight (through economics)?
Schelling, T C (1988) *Choice and Consequence*, p. 85. Cambridge, MA: Harvard University Press

Thaler, R H and Sunstein, C R (2009) *Nudge: Improving Decisions about Health, Wealth, and Happiness*, p. 44. London: Penguin

What is the optimal number of children to have?
Becker, G S and Lewis, H G (1973) "On the interaction between the quantity and quality of children", *Journal of Political Economy*, vol. 81, no. 2, part 2, p. 279

CHAPTER 2
If I enjoy drinking beer, how much should I drink?
Keynes, J M (1965) "We are all Keynesians now", *Time*, 31 December, vol. 86, no. 27, p. 74

Marshall, A (1890) *Principles of Economics*, 8th edition, ch. 3. London: Macmillan

Can I trust a second-hand car salesman?
Akerlof, G A (1970) "The market for lemons: Quality uncertainty and the market mechanism", *Quarterly Journal of Economics*, vol. 84, no. 3, pp. 488–500

Tabarrok, A and Cowen T (2015) "The end of asymmetric information", *Cato Unbound*, 6 April. Accessed online 18 June 2017: https://www.cato-unbound.org/2015/04/06/alex-tabarrok-tyler-cowen/end-asymmetric-information

How do we best manage common resources?
Fennell, L A (2011) "Ostrom's law: property rights in the commons", *International Journal of the Commons*, vol. 5, no. 1, p. 9

Hardin, G (1968) "The tragedy of the commons", *Science*, vol. 162, pp. 1243–1248. Accessed online 26 June 2017: http://dieoff.org/page95.htm

Ostrom, E (2016 [1990]) *Governing the Commons*. Cambridge, UK: Cambridge University Press

Bibliography

Should I pay to go to the front of the line?

Sandel, M (2013) *What Money Can't Buy: The Moral Limits of Markets*, p. 39. New York: Farrar, Straus and Giroux

How much should we give to charity?

Bauer, P, quoted in Anon (2002) "A voice for the poor", *The Economist*, 2 May Accessed online 20 June 2017: http://www.economist.com/node/1109786

Becker, G S (1976) *The Economic Approach to Human Behavior*, p. 273. Chicago, IL: University of Chicago Press

Landsburg, S E (1997) "Giving your all", *Slate Magazine*, 10 January

Should I give a gift or money for a Christmas present?

Friedman, M and Friedman, R (1990) *Free to Choose: A Personal Statement*. Boston, MA: Houghton Mifflin Harcourt

Niemietz, K (2015) "Don't let anti-consumerists kill your Christmas spirit", 11 December. London: Institute of Economic Affairs. Accessed online 18 June 2017: https://iea.org.uk/blog/dont-let-anti-consumerists-kill-your-christmas-spirit

Waldfogel, J (1993) "The deadweight loss of Christmas", *American Economic Review*, vol. 83, no. 5, pp. 1328–1336

Should I favour buying local goods?

Interview with Friedrich Hayek (1980), *Silver & Gold Report* (1980), vol. 5, no. 20, late October, quoted on Wikiquote. Accessed online 17 July 2017: https://en.wikiquote.org/wiki/Friedrich_Hayek

Smith, A (1993 [1776]) *The Wealth of Nations*, Book IV, Ch. II, p. 293. Oxford: Oxford University Press

Roberts, R (2011) "Don't follow the money", *Cafe Hayek*, 25 February. Accessed online 19 June 2017: http://cafehayek.com/2011/02/dont-follow-the-money.html

How can I get a good deal when shopping?

Harford, T (2012) *The Undercover Economist*. Oxford: Oxford University Press

CHAPTER 3
Should I go to college/university?

Becker, G (2002) "The age of human capital". In E P Lazear (ed.) *Education in the Twenty-first Century*, p. 8. Stanford, CA: Hoover Institution Press

Keynes, J M, as quoted in Rosten, C (1979) *Infinite Riches: Gems from a Lifetime of Reading*, p. 165. New York: McGraw-Hill

Thurow, L C (1994) "Education and falling wages", *New England Journal of Public Policy*, vol. 10, no. 1, Article 6

Is it worth taking a promotion if it involves working long hours?

Peter, L J and Hull, R (2011) *The Peter Principle: Why Things Always Go Wrong*. New York: Harper Business

How do I motivate my fellow workers?

Ariely, D (2016) *Payoff: The Hidden Logic that Shapes our Motivations*, pp. 27. New York: Simon & Schuster

Lazear, E (1985) "Incentive contracts", NBER working paper no. 1917, National Bureau of Economic Research. Accessed online 26 June 2017: http://www.nber.org/papers/w1917.pdf

Do I benefit or suffer from immigration?

Friedman, M quoted in Bowman, S (2013) "Milton Friedman's objection to immigration", 3 July. London: Adam Smith Institute. Accessed online 13 June 2017: https://www.adamsmith.org/blog/economics/milton-friedman-s-objection-to-immigration

Samuelson, P (1973) *Economics*. New York: McGraw-Hill. p. 573

Should I give up my secure job and work for myself?

Levine, R and Rubinstein, Y (2013) "Smart and illicit: Who becomes an entrepreneur and does it pay?", CEP discussion paper no. 1237, August. London: Centre for Economic Performance

How can I get a pay rise?

Bowles, H R, Babcock, L and Lai, L (2007) "Social incentives for gender differences in the propensity to initiate negotiations: Sometimes it does hurt to ask", *Organizational Behavior and Human Decision Processes*, vol. 103, no. 1, p. 84

Bibliography

Smith, A (1993 [1776]) *The Wealth of Nations*, Book I, Ch. VIII, p. 65. Oxford: Oxford University Press

How can I be a good manager of people?
Ariely, D (2016) *Payoff: The Hidden Logic that Shapes our Motivations*, p. 67. New York: Simon & Schuster

Kahneman, D (2015) *Thinking, Fast and Slow.* New York: Farrar, Straus & Giroux

Should I run my business just for profit?
Friedman, M (2002) *Capitalism and Freedom*, p. 133. Chicago, IL: University of Chicago Press

CHAPTER 4
How do I beat the market?
Kahneman, D (2011) "Don't blink! The hazards of confidence", *The New York Times,* 22 October. Accessed online 19 June 2017: http://www.nytimes.com/2011/10/23/magazine/dont-blink-the-hazards-of-confidence.html

Keynes, J M (2007), quoted in Braham, L (2007) "The Short Sell Made Simple", *Business Week*, no. 4035, p. 100

How do I survive inflation?
Friedman, M (2006) "Milton Friedman's Last Lunch", Forbes. Accessed online 7 June 2017: https://www.forbes.com/forbes/2006/1211/056a.html

Keynes, J M (1919) *The Economic Consequences of the Peace*, p. 235. New York: Harcourt, Brace, & Howe

Mises, L von (1990) *Economic Freedom and Interventionism: An Anthology of Articles and Essays*, p. 86. Irvington, NY: Foundation for Economic Education

How can I make my small business more profitable?
Harford, T (2010) *The Undercover Economist*, p. 39. London: Hachette UK

Schumpeter, J A (1950) *Capitalism, Socialism, and Democracy*, 3rd edition, p. 83. New York: Harper & Brothers

How much I should put into retirement savings?
Carnegie, A (1889) "Wealth", *North American Review*, vol. 148, no. 391, p. 664.

Kotlikoff, L, quoted in Kadlec, D (2012) "Are you saving too much? No, really", *Time*, 20 June. Accessed online 20 June 2017: http://business.time.com/2012/06/20/are-you-saving-too-much-no-really/

How do I avoid getting caught by financial bubbles?
Buffett, W (2010) "Interview with Warren Buffett", *CNBC*, 5 August. Accessed online 19 June 2017: http://www.cnbc.com/id/26982338

How much personal debt should I take on?
Smith, A (2010 [1759]) *The Theory of Moral Sentiments*, Section III, Ch. 1, p. 7. London: Penguin Classics

CHAPTER 5
Should I vote for a political party that promises to cut my income taxes?
Krugman, P (2009) *The Conscience of a Liberal*, ch. 6. New York: W W Norton & Co.

Office of Public Affairs (2003) "250 economists endorse President Bush's jobs and growth plan", 12 February. Washington, DC: US Department of the Treasury. Accessed online 19 June 2017: https://www.treasury.gov/press-center/press-releases/Pages/js28.aspx

Should I boycott goods made in sweatshop factories?
Pollin, R quoted in Miller, J (2003) "Why economists are wrong about sweatshops and the antisweatshop movement", *Challenge*, vol. 46, no. 1, p. 95

Sachs, J and Levinson, M quoted in Veseth, M (ed.) (2002) *The Rise of the Global Economy*, p. 379). Abingdon: Taylor & Francis

Should I support government subsidies for a local firm facing bankruptcy?
Friedman, M and Friedman, R D (1985) *Tyranny of the Status Quo*, p. 115. Harmondsworth: Penguin

Krueger, A quoted in Guida, J and (2015) "How the auto bailout helped save the economy", *The New York Times*, 5 March. Accessed online 21 June 2017: https://op-talk.blogs.nytimes.com/2015/03/05/how-the-auto-bailout-helped-save-the-economy/

Bibliography

Will I be better off with tariffs on imports?
Mankiw, G N (2015) "Economists actually agree on this: the wisdom of free trade", *The New York Times*, 24 April. Accessed online 24 June 2017: https://www.nytimes.com/2015/04/26/upshot/economists-actually-agree-on-this-point-the-wisdom-of-free-trade.html

Should I welcome parking charges in my street and city?
Smith, A (1999 [1776]) *The Wealth of Nations*, Book V, Chapter II, Part II, p. 927. London: Penguin.

Should I worry about my government getting into debt?
Krugman, P (2012) *End This Depression Now!* New York: W W Norton & Co.

Keynes, J M (1936) *The General Theory of Employment, Interest and Money*, Book 4, Chapter 16, p. 220. London: Palgrave Macmillan

Should we worry about rising inequality?
Baumol, W J (2007) "On income distribution and growth", *Journal of Policy Modeling*, vol. 29, no. 4, pp. 545–548

Should healthcare be private or public?
Hayek, F A (1994 [1944]) *The Road to Serfdom*, p. 131. Chicago, IL: University of Chicago Press

Krugman, P (2017) "Health care fundamentals", *The New York Times*, 18 January. Accessed online 14 June 2017: https://krugman.blogs.nytimes.com/2017/01/18/health-care-fundamentals/

DIAGRAM SOURCES
Page 130
US Bureau of Labor Statistics, CPI: Purchasing Power of the Consumer Dollar. Accessed online 14 August 2017 from FRED (Federal Reserve Bank of St. Louis): https://fred.stlouisfed.org/series/CUUR0000SA0R

Page 142
Shiller, R J (2017) "Online data – Price to earnings ratio". Accessed online 19 June 2017: http://www.multpl.com/shiller-pe/

Index

A

acquisition utility 73, *74*, 82
Adam Smith Institute (ASI) 78
Adams, J Stacy 98
adhocracy 114
Adidas-Salomon 157
adverse selection 55
aid curse 67
Akerlof, George 54–6 *passim*, 57,
  95, 96, 108, 122, 123, 154, 156
alcohol comsumption 50–3
altruism 13, 67, 70
Anderson, William L 55
Andreoni, James 67, 69, 70, 83
Animal Spirits (Akerlof, Shiller) 123
applied economics 6
appreciation 98
Ariely, Dan 19, 21, 80, 82, 95,
  96–7, 98, 104, 106, 112, 113, 115,
  132, 135, 144
The Armchair Economist
  (Landsburg) 38
Arnold, Denis 157
Atkinson, J W 97
austerity 35, 176

B

Babcock, Linda 109
bad behaviour 25
bankruptcy 158–61, *159*
Baron, David P 118
Barro, Robert 169, 170
Bauer, Peter 67, 68
Baumol, William 36, 177, 179
Becker, Gary 6, 7, 14–17 *passim*,
  18, 32, 33, 35, 40, 44–7, 63, 66–70
  passim, 86–7, 90, 108–9, 111, 116,
  118, 169, 171
beer drinking 50–1, *51*, *52*, 53, 76
"Behaving Badly" (Montier) 122
behaviour:
  consumer 33
  illogical 33
  influencing 43
  risk-averse 28–9, 30
  risk-loving 28–9, 30
behavioural economics 6–7, 25,
  40–1, 42–3, 53, 81, 83, 134, 137
behavioural factors 114–15
behavioural theory 19
belonging 97, *97*
Benartzi, Shlomo 136, 137
Bennis, Warren G 112, 114
Bentham, Jeremy 14, 15, 19, 22,
  50, 53
Bernheim, Douglas 83
Bernoulli, Daniel 28–9
van Beukering, Pieter 36, 39
Bhagwati, Jagdish 67, 68, 154, 156
birth rates 44–5, 100
Blanchflower, David 104, 105
Blasi, Joseph 96
Blinder, Alan 126, 128
Borjas, George 99, 102
Bourdieu, Pierre 14, 18, 86, 89
Bourne, Ryan 71, 75

Boushey, Heather 91, 93
Bowles, Hannah Riley 109
Boyce, Chris 93
Boyle, David 77
brand differentiation 134
Branson, Richard 89
Brickman, Philip 91
budget deficits 175–6
Buffett, Warren 125, 140
Bulow, Jeremy 126, 128
Bush, George W 150, 151
"Buy American, Hire American"
  (US executive order) 76
buy local 76–9, 80

C

Cambodia 156
Campbell, Donald 91
cancer research 68
cannabis tourists 172
capital flight 176
Capital in the Twenty-First Century
  (Piketty) 177
capitalism:
  essential fact about 133
  self-interest 10–11
  soul-destroying nature of 94
  wage slavery caused by 110
Caplan, Bryan 99, 100
car supermarkets 56
Card, David 99, 101, 102
cardinal utility 52
Care International 68
Carnegie, Andrew 138, 139
Carneiro, Pedro 86
Case, Karl 140, 143
Case–Shiller home price index 143
cash efficiency 75
Cato Institute 182
central banks 90, 100, 136, 139,
  142, 176
The Challenge of Affluence (Offer) 22
Chang, Ha-Joon 144, 145, 147,
  162, 163
charitable donations 67–70, *69*
chartist strategies 123
child labour 157
children 44–7, 139
choice *79*, 81, *183*
  default 135
  environment affects 42–3, *42*
  mindless 43
choice architecture 43
choice aversion 81
Chomsky, Noam 108, 110
Christmas *73*, *74*, 145
  debt *146*
  market failure 71
  presents 71–5
  by spreadsheet 72, 74
civic virtue 66
classical economics 10
Clinton, Bill 183
Coase, Ronald 23, 24, 27
Coase theorem 23–4, 25, 26
cognitive behaviour 83

cognitive bias 83
Colbert, Jean-Baptiste 44
"cold state" 40, 83
collective action 58–9
common land 15, 58, *59*, 61, 62
Common Pool Resource (CPR) 59
common resources 58–62
community economics 77
community welfare 79
comparative advantage, theory of
  112, 162
compensation 23, 24
competitive labour markets, theory
  of 109
conditionally cooperative 25
conflict resolution 23–4, *23*, 25
consumption 20, 52, 55, 59, 61, 62,
  71, 146
  conspicuous 144–5
  maximizing 91
  psychology of 80
  smoothing 136, 137, *138–9*, 147
contrarian attitude 123, 140
Cordell, Larry 90
cost, utility vs 46
cost of living 126, 156
cost-push factors 128
Cowen, Tyler 54, 56, 57, 165, 167,
  168
creative destruction 132, 133, 158
creativity 89
credit bubbles:
  1720 140
  1912–13 145
  1990s 140, 142
  2000s 118, 142, 145
credit crunch (2007–8) 140, 141, 143
crime reduction 86
criminal actions, cost/benefit
  analysing of 14–15, 17–18
crowding out 173
cutting losses 133
Cyclically Adjusted Price-to-
  Earnings (CAPE) ratio 143

D

dead capital 61
deadweight welfare loss 65, 71, 150
debt deflation 141
decision costs 81
decision-making 83
default choice 135
default options 81
deficit 150
deficit spending 175, 176, *176*
degrees, costs and benefits of 86–7,
  87, 88, 89, 90
delegation 112, *113*
demerit good 52
democracy, foreign aid undermines 68
depressed economy 130
Desrochers, Pierre 78
Devarajan, Shanta 182
DeYoung, Robert 147
dieting 40–3, *41*
diminishing returns 21, 22, 51, 91,

Index

96, 179
discounting *134*, 142
disputes, *see* conflict resolution
division of labour 63, 112
Djankov, Simeon 67–8
Dobridge, Christine L 146
dot-com crash (1999) 140, *142*
Doughnut Economics (Raworth) 57, 59
Dow Jones Industrial Average 142–3
drinking, *see* alcohol comsumption
Drucker, Peter F 108, 132
drugs 105, 169–72, *170, 171*
Dubner, Stephen J 35, 44, 64, 105
Dustmann, Christian 100

E

economic development 45, 67
economic downturn (2009–16) 126
economic efficiency 110
economic growth 6, 78, 150, 153, 173, 175, 177, 178
   psychological and social influences impact on 6–7, 114–15
The Economic Naturalist (Frank) 80
economic patriotism 78
economic theory, clashes in society with 35
economic value, quantifying 32
economic welfare 10, 11, 15, 78, 79
economics:
   Austrian school of 128
   classical school of 10, 116, 144
   "dismal science" 19, 47, 91
   "happiness" 19, 91
   laissez-faire 128, 158
   of reciprocity 25, 57
   trickle-down 11, *12*, 150
The Economics of Waste (Porter) 36
The Economics of Welfare (Pigou) 13
economist's economist 108
Edison, Thomas 89
education 46, 86, 150
effective delegation 112
efficiency wage theory 96, 108
efficient market hypothesis 122, 123, 125, 141, 142
"eight design principles" 59
80/20 rule 114
Einstein, Albert 47
Emons, Winand 56
employment 91–4
"The End of Asymmetric Information" (Tabarrok, Cowen) 56
endowment effect 25, 30
energy-saving 32–5, *33, 34*
entitlement 25
entrepreneurship 89, 90, 102, 104, 107, 150, 154
equality 22, 66
equity 167
Equity theory 98
Erb, Claude B 126, 129
Evans, Peter B 154, 156
exit strategy 133
expectation 22, 35, 129

expected value, law of 30
expected value theory 28
external costs 13, 165
externalities, theory of 165

F

fads 40
fair trade 135, *135*
fair value 57
fairness 98, 167
"Fairness and Retaliation: The Economics of Reciprocity" (Fehr) 98
Fama, Eugene 122, 125
family, optimal size of 44
Fehr, Ernst 23, 25, 26, 95, 98
Feldstein, Martin 126, 127, 130
Fennell, Lee Anne 59, 61
fiat currency 128–9
financial bubbles 123, 124, 125, 140–3
financial crashes 124
   (1987) *142*
   (2008) 175, 176
financial incentives 95–6, *95*, 140–3
financial instability hypothesis 141
financial penalties 43
financial trading 122–5
Fishback, Ayelet 65
Fisher equation 126, *126*
Fisher, Irving 50, 52–3, 126, 127, 140, 141, 143, 169, 172
fishing quotas 58
Fisman, Raymond 17
flat-white economy 102
food miles 78, *78*
food stamps 179
foreign aid 67–8
"Four Ways to Spend Money" (Friedman) 72
Frank, Robert H 10, 11, 80
Franklin, Benjamin 32
Frattini, Tommaso 100
Freakonomics (Levitt, Dubner) 35, 44, 105
free-market economics 7, 11, 12–13, 93, 110, 151, *159*, 178
free-rider problem 58, 67
free trade 76, 77, 79, 162, 163
Freeman, Richard B 86, 90, 91, 92, 95, 96
Frey, Bruno S 19, 21, 91, 94
Friedberg, Rachel 101
Friedman, Benjamin 91, 93, 94
Friedman, Gerald 104, 106, 107
Friedman, Milton 7, 10, 12, 28, 29, 58, 61, 71, 72, 75, 99–100, 104, 107–10 *passim*, 116–19 *passim*, 126–31 *passim*, 144–7 *passim*, 150, 152, 158, 160–2, 164, 169, 171–2, 177–83 *passim*, *181*
Friedman, Rose 72, 160
Friedman–Savage utility function 29
Friedman, Thomas 106

G

Galbraith, John Kenneth 10, 11
gambling 28–31

Gandhi, Mahatma 21
Gates, Bill 89, 105
GDP (Gross Domestic Product) 78, 100, 102, *141*, 144, 173, 175–6, 181
General Theory of Employment, Interest and Money (Keynes) 6
The Gift: Forms and Functions of Exchange in Archaic Societies (Mauss) 72
gift-giving 69–70, *69*, 71–5, *73, 74*
The Gift: How the Creative Spirit Transforms the World (Hyde) 72
gig economy 106–7
Gilded Age 11
global warming *45*, 47, 78
globalization 79, 86, 99, 162
The Golden Constant (Jastram) 129
The Golden Dilemma (Erb) 129
Governing the Commons (Ostrom) 58
government borrowing 173
government intervention 58
government regulation 13, 62
government subsidies 158–61, *160*
Graeber, David 144, 146
Great Depression 6, 34, 141, 160, 173
green issues 32–5, *33, 34*, 36–9, *37, 38*, 62, 71, 77, 78, 167
Greenspan, Alan 99, 100, 140, 142
Gresham, Thomas 54, 55
Gresham's Law 55
Gridlock Economy (Heller) 62
"Growth in a Time of Debt" (Rogoff) 175
Gruber, Jonathan 23, 24

H

Haber, Lawrence J 111
Haldane, Andy 136, 139
halo effect 118
Hamilton, Barton H 105
Hanson, Gordon 99, 101
happiness 19–22, *19*, 30, *79*
   and beer consumption 50, *51*
   and income *19*, 21–2, 30–1
   index 153
   stability of 91
   and wealth 21–2
Happiness – A Revolution in Economics (Frey) 21
Hardin, Garrett 58, 62
Harford, Tim 80, 81, 132, 134, 135
harmony 34–5
Hartman, Laura 157
Hayek, Friedrich 10, 12, 76, 78, 150, 151, 158, 180, 182
health care 65, 86, 100, 150, 153, *170*, 179–83, *181, 183*
Heller, Michael 58, 62
herd behaviour/instinct 140
Hicks, John Richard 50, 52
Hierarchy of Needs (Maslow) 97
Hirschman, Albert O 132, 133
Hobbes, Thomas 14, 17
horse and sparrow theory 11
Horwitz, Steven 132, 133
hot–cold states, theory of 40

Index

"hot state" 40, 83
housing market 127, 143
Huhtala, Anni 37, 39
human capital, theory of 86, 89, 104, 111, 145
Hyde, Lewis 72
hyperinflation 127, 128, *129*

I

immigration 99–102, *101*
imperfect decisions 83
import tariffs 76, 162–4, *164*
impulse-buying 83
incentive 35, 40, *108*
income 138, 145, *152* (*see also* wage(s))
  bonuses 97
  effect 92
  happiness affected by *19*, 21–2, 30–1
  and promotion 91–4
  utility of money affected by 29
income–leisure trade-off 94
index fund 123
industrial efficiency 6
inequality 66, 177–9, *178*
inflation 6, 126–31, *126*, *130*
information asymmetry 54, 55, 71–2, 75
innovation 101, 102
Institute of Economic Affairs 75
insurance 28–31, 54, 81
interested sophistry 76
"The Intimate Contest for Self-Command" (Schelling) 42
intrinsic value 37–8, 65
invisible hand 117
irrational behaviour, rationality of 81–2, *82*
irrational exuberance 142, 143

J

Jastram, Roy 126, 129
Jensen, Michael C 95, 122, 123
Jevons, William Stanley 10, 50, 52, 79, 132, 134
Jobs, Steve 105
The Joyless Economy (Scitovsky) 20
justice 24–5

K

Kahneman, Daniel 7, 23, 25, 28, 30, 40–1, 43, 80, 83, 112, 114, 115, 122, 125, 136, 137, 180
Karlan, Dean 40
Kennedy, Duncan 25
Keynes, John Maynard 6, 7, 7, 32, 34, 50–3 *passim*, 67, 70, 89–93 *passim*, 122–7 *passim*, 136, 142, 162, 163, 173–5, 177
Keynesian theory 175, 176
Kicking Away the Ladder (Chang) 163
King, Mervyn 136
Kinnaman, Thomas 36, 37, 38, 39
Kirzner, Israel 55
Kitzmuller, Markus 118, 119
Knight, Frank 10, 11

"Knowing about Knowledge: A Subjectivist View of the Role of Information" (Kirzner) 55
knowledge economy 108, 113
Kosfeld, Michael 98
Kotlikoff, Laurence 136, 138, 139
Kristof, Nicholas 154, 156
Krueger, Alan 158, 159, 160
Krugman, Paul 126, 130, 144, 145, 150, 151, 152, 153, 154, 157, 158, 160, 173, 176, 177, 179, 180, 183
Kruse, Douglas 96
Kuznets, Simon 154, 155

L

La, Lei 109
Laffer, Arthur 150, 151, 153
Laffer curve 151, *151*
landfill 36, 37
Landry, Craig 69, 70
Landsburg, Steven 36, 38–9, 67, 68, 69, 70, 76, 77, 78
Lang, Tim 78
Lazear, Edward 95, 96, 98, 104, 107
leadership skills 112–15, *115*
"lemon" or "peach"? 54, 55, 56
Levin, Jonathan 34, 35
Levine, Ross 104, 105, 106, 107
Levitt, Steven 40, 42, 44, 104, 105
Levitt, Theodore 112, 113, 114, 115
Lewis, H Gregg 44, 45, 46, 47
libertarian economics 12, 39, 55, 99, 182
life-cycle hypothesis 136, 137, 139
liquidity trap 126, 130
List, Friedrich 162, 163
living wage 156
Lloyd, William Forster 15, 58
Local Ownership Import Substituting (LOIS) 77
locavore 77, 78
The Locavore's Dilemma: In Praise of the 10,000-mile Diet (Desrochers, Shimizu) 78
Loewenstein, George 40
long hours 91–4
loss-aversion effect 41, 138
lotteries 28, 30
lump of labour fallacy 100
Lynch, Peter 124, 125

M

McClelland, David 97
MacCoun, Robert J 172
Machlup, Fritz 77
McKinsey Quarterly 135
MacWilliams, Douglas 102
Malcomson , James 97
Malkiel, Burton 122, 123
Malthus, Thomas Robert 44, *45*, 47
management skills 112–15, *115*
Mankiw, Greg 150, 153, 162, 163, 164
Manville, Michael 168
marginal benefits 133–4
marginal cost 19, 71
marginal revenue product (MRP)

108, 109
Marginal Revolution 56
marginal substitution theory 19
marginal utility theory 19, 20, 53, 64, 71, 79, 91
market equilibrium 156
market imperfections 83
"The Market for Lemons: Quality Uncertainty and the Market Mechanism" (Akerlof) 54
marketing strategies 80
markets 25–6, *26*, 109
Marshall, Alfred 7, 19, 50, 52, 71, 132, 134, 136
Marx, Karl 7, 10–11, 91, 94, 104, 105
Maslow, Abraham 95, 97
Maslow's triangle *97*
materialism 13, 22
Mauus, Marcel 70, 72, 73
Maybaum, Lloyd 65
Meckling, William 95
Mejía, Daniel 170
Menger, Carl 19, 22, 50, 51, 91
mental accounting 33, 83, 134
mental health 93, 171
mental myopia 180
mercantilism 44
Merton, Robert K 92
microbanking 147
migration 99, 100–2, *101*
Miguel, Edward 17
Milgrom, Paul 34, 112, 113
Mill, John Stuart 50
Miller, John 155
Mincer, Jacob 86, 87
Minsky, Hyman 140, 141
Minsky moment 141, *141*
Miron, Jeffrey 169, 170
Misbehaving: the Making of Behavioural Economics (Thaler) 134
von Mises, Ludwig 10, 12, 13, 126, 128, 130, 144, 145, 177
Modern Monetary Theory (MMT) 176
Modigliani, Franco 136
monetarism 129–30
money, case for spending 19
money supply 129
monopsony 109
Montier, James 122
Monty Python 104
Moore, Mark H 169, 171
moral hazard 68
morality 50, 65, 68, 144
motivation 95–8, *95*, 132
Munger, Mike 36, 39
Murphy's Law 31
myopic loss aversion 124
The Mystery of Capital (de Soto) 61

N

Nash equilibrium 110
Nash, John Forbes Jr 108, 110
National Day of Conception 44
National Debt 173–6
National Minimum Wage 106
Need for Achievement Theory 97

Index

negative externalities 13, 53
negative utility 20
neighbours, disputes between 23–7
neoclassical theory 21, 53, 57
net economic welfare 79
net gain 164
New Economics Foundation (NEF) 77
Newton, Isaac 47
Niemietz, Kristian 74
Nixon, Richard 170
non-sovereign debt 176
Nudge: Improving Decisions About Health, Wealth, and Happiness (Thaler, Sunstein) 43

O

Oberholzer-Gee, Felix 63–4, 66
Obloj, Tomasz 95, 96
O'Donoghue, Ted 137
Offer, Avner 22
de Oliveira, M Mendes 90
"100 Ways to Fight Obesity" 42
opportunity cost 45
optimisation 58
optimism bias 53, 114, 122
Ostrom, Elinor 58, 59, 60, 61, 62
Ostrom's Law 59
Oswald, Andrew 93, 104, 105
"out of sight, out of mind" 83
The Overeducated American (Freeman) 90
Owen, John D 92, 93

P

paradoxical behaviour 32–3
parenting skills 86
Pareto efficiency outcome 24
Pareto, Vilfredo 23, 24, 112, 114
parking 14–18, *15*, 165–8, *167*, *168*
party politics 150–3
patience, how to obtain 65
pay rises 108–11
payday loans 146
perfect altruism 67
permanent income hypothesis 145
personal debt 144–7, *145*
personal opinions 53
personal satisfaction 66
personnel economics 95
perspective 33–4
pessimism 47, 110, 115
Peter, Laurence J 94
Peter Principle 94
philanthropy 70
Pigou, Arthur 10, 13, 165, 167, 177, 179
Piketty, Thomas 177, 178, 179
Pollin, Robert 154, 156
pollution 36, 71, 77, 165, 167
population growth 44–5, 47
Porter, Richard C 36
positive externalities 74, 79
positivity 53
poverty 68, 155, 179
Powell, Benjamin 154, 156
pre-commitment strategies 41, *41*, 42

Predictably Irrational (Ariely) 144
present bias 21, 40, 137
price:
  discrimination 64, 80
  mark-up 80–1
  sensitivity 80
  targeting 134
  theory 63
price-comparison websites 81
The Price of Leisure (Owen) 92
price-to-earnings ratio 124, 141, 142–3, *142*
principal-agent problem 95
principle of utility 19, 50
Pritchett, Lant 99, 102
private ownership 58, *59*, 61, 62
probability 17, 28
procrastination 137, 139
procreation, incentives for 44
productivity 86, 89, 93, 95, 96, 108, 110, 111, 115
profit maximization 10, *26*, 95, 116–19, *117*, *119*, 132–5
profit-sharing 96
Prohibition 169–70, *169*, *170*, *171*, 172
promotion 91–4, *95*
property rights 23, 61
prospect theory *29*, 30, 31
protectionism 76, 77, 79, 163, *163*, *164*
The Protestant Ethic and the Spirit of Capitalism (Weber) 144
prudence 136

Q

quantitative easing (QE) 129
queue-jumping 63–6, *64*, *65*
"quit tomorrow" option 41

R

Ramsey, Frank P 67
A Random Walk Down Wall Street (Malkiel) 123
random walk theory 123, *123*
Rangel, Antonio 83
rational:
  investment 142
  self-interest, *see* self-interest
rational choice theory 18, 32–5 *passim*, 40, *41*, 60, 63
Raworth, Kate 57, 59
Reagan, Ronald 110, 150, 151
reality check 24
recession 173, 175
reciprocal cooperation 25
Recognizing Public Value (Moore) 171
recycling 36–9, *37*, *38*
regulation, *see* government regulation
Reinhardt , Forest L 119
Reinhart, Carmen 140, 173
repugnant transaction 65
reputational effects 57
resources *45*, 71
responsibility 91, 92, 94, *95*, 97, 98, *107*, 112, *113*

corporate 118–19
  delegation of 114
  social 57, 114, 116–19, *119*
retirement 91, 136–9, *138–9*
Ricardian trade theory 162
Ricardo, David 6, 10, 79, 108, 112, 126, 144, 162, 164, 173, *176*
risk 20, 28–9, 107
The Road to Serfdom (Hayek) 182
Robbins, Lionel 126, 127
Roberts, Harry 122
Roberts, Russ 76, 77
Robin Hood Tax 65
Robinson, Joan 108, 109, 111, 162, 163
Robinson, Kenneth 89
Rogoff, Kenneth 140, 173, 175
Romalis, John 40
Roth, Alvin 63, 65
Rothschild, Michael 180, 181
rotten kid theorem 46
Rubinstein, Yona 105
Russia 127

S

Sachs, Jeffrey 67, 154, 155
Saiz, Albert 102
salary, *see* income; wage(s)
Samuelson, Paul 99, *101*, 102, 103, 150, 153
Sandel, Michael 23, 25–6, 63, 64, 65, 66
satisfaction 19, 20, 52
Savage, Leonard 28, 29
scarcity value 90, 114
Schelling, Thomas 40, 41–2, 43
Schloss, D F 99, 100
Schumacher, E F 71, 76, 78, 116, 117, 119
Schumpeter, Joseph 132, 133, 158, 160
Scitovsky, Tibor 19, 20, 21, 22, 91, 93, 94
Scroogenomics (Waldfogel) 71
second-hand car sales 54–7, *54*, 55, *56*
self-actualization 97, *97*, 106
self-control 42, 43, 65, 146
self-employment 104–7, *104*, *107*
self-esteem 92, 97, *97*
self-interest 10, 11–12, 13, 59, 67, 76
self-organized systems 59
self-regulation 58–9, 61
self-servers 57
self-sufficiency 79
selfishness 10–13
Sen, Amartya 177, 179
Shapiro, Carl 95, 96
S*hared Capitalism at Work* (Freeman) 96
shared resources 58
sharing 61–2, *61*
Shefrin, Hersh 136, 137
Sheldon, George 56
Shiller, Robert 122, 123, 140, 142, 143, 147
Shimizu, Hiroko 78"Shop with a

Conscience Consumer Guide" 156
shopping 80–3
Shoup, Donald 165, 167, 168
Shoven, John B 126, 128
Shuman, Michael 77
signalling theory 56, 89
sin tax 170
Skidelsky, Robert 89
skilled consumption 20
Small is Beautiful (Schumacher) 78
SMarT 138
Smith, Adam 6, 7, 10, 12, 63, 76,
78–9, 83, 95–6, 108–12 *passim*,
116–17, 144–5, 165–6, 173, *176*
Smith, Vernon L 80, 81
Smithers, Andrew 123
social acclaim 68
social mobility 179
social norms 35
social responsibility 57, 114,
116–19, *119*
social welfare 70
socially efficient level 58, 167
de Soto, Hernando 58, 61, 62
South Sea Bubble (1720) 140
Sowell, Thomas 177, 178
special offers 82, *82*, 83
Spence, Michael 54, 56, 86, 89, 90
spillover effects 13
split personality 83
spontaneous cooperation 58
spontaneous order 13
Standard & Poor (S&P) 125
starvation 68
status 92
status quo bias 81
Stevenson, Betsey 19, 22
Stiglitz, Joseph 95, 96, 108, 109,
116, 117, 150, 153, 162, 164, 177,
178, 179, 180, 181
Stockman, David 150
student debt 86, 90, *90*
subjective perceptions 53
substitution effect 92, 94
Summers, Larry 158, 159, 161
sunk cost 19, 133
Sunstein, Cass 40, 43, 80, 81
supersizing 81, *81*
supply side 110, 152, 153
sustainability 62
sweatshops 154–7, *155*

T
Tabarrok, Alex 54, 56, 57
Tanner, Michael D 180, 182
Taubman, Paul 171, 172
tax revenue 100, 116, 118, 131, 150–
3, *151*, *152*, 161, *169*, 170–1, 179
teams 108, 113
technology, slow progress of *45*
Thaler, Richard 7, 19, 23–5, 28,
31–2, *33*, 35, 40, 43, 71, 73, 80–3,
122, 124, 132, 134–7, 139
Thatcher, Margaret 110
The Theory of the Leisure Class
(Veblen) 92
thinking, outside-the-box 89
This Time is Different (Reinhart,
Rogoff) 140
Thoma, Mark 158, 165, 167
Thornton, Mark 169, 170
Thorpe, Kenneth E 183
thrift 134–6, 173
Thurow, Lester 86, 87, 88
"time is money" 32
tipping 35
trade deficit 76
trade quotas 76
trades union movement 110, 111, *111*
"The Tragedy of the Commons"
15, 58, *59*
training, on-the-job 87
transaction utility 73, *74*, 134
Trichet, Jean-Claude 176
Trump, Donald 76, 151
trust 61, 72–3, 98, 112, 113
Tulip Mania (1637) 140
TV viewing, boredom generated
by 20
Tversky, Amos 28, 30, 122, 124,
136, 137

U
The Undercover Economist
(Harford) 134
util 52
utilitarianism 15, 17–18, 50, 52
utility:
function 29
maximization 10, 19–20, 30, 32,
52, 58, 66, 71
of money 21, 29, 136

V
value judgments 53
Veblen, Thorstein 91, 92, 144
voice strategy 133

W
wage(s) (*see also* income; pay rises):
determination, theory of 108
and immigration 99, 101, 102
living 156
minimum 106
premium 90
restraint 111
slavery 110
sweatshop 155, 156, 157
Waldfogel, Joel 71, 72, 75
Wall Street Crash (1929) 140, 141,
142, *142*
Walras, Léon 108
Wansink, Brian 40, 42–3
waste management 37, 39
Watson, Philip 79
The Wealth of Nations (Smith) 10,
112, 165
Weber, Max 91, 92, 144
weight control 40–3, *41*
Weintraub, Robert E 44
welfare benefits 99, 178
welfare economics 100
"The Welfare Economics of 'Buy
Local'" (Winfree, Watson) 79
Wicksell, Knut 108
Wilde, Oscar 72
Winfree, Jason 79
"wisdom of the crowds" 140
Wiseman, Clark 39
work–life balance 92–4
worker empowerment 114
Worstall, Tim 76, 78
Wray, L Randall 173, 176

X
Xenophon 41

Y
Yellen, Janet 108
Yunus, Muhammad 144, 147

Z
zero interest rates 130
zero retirement savings 136
zero utility 72
Zuluaga, Diego 73, 75

Acknowledgments

Many thanks to the team at Octopus for helping to put the book together, especially Trevor Davies, Polly Poulter, Alison Wormleighton, Mairi Sutherland, Ella Mclean, Grace Helmer and Sarah Kulasek-Boyd. Thanks also to Gareth Southwell for his characterful illustrations.